PRAISE

Beyond Self-Defense

"In my forty years of martial art experience, I have taken and taught countless self-defense courses. Shihan Michelle's Self Offense program is by far the best I've ever experienced. Its comprehensive and practical approach makes it very accessible for people from all walks of life no matter what their experience level. Plain and simple the woman knows what she's doing. Listen to her! (And buy this book!)"

— SHIHAN GENE DUNN, founder of Gene Dunn's Shotokan Karate and Brooklyn Brazilian Jiu Jitsu; 6th Dan, Shotokan; 4th Dan, Renzo Gracie Jiu Jitsu; Shodan Judo; author; and artist

"Shihan Michelle has a passion for helping people make positive changes. . . . She is offering suggestions about how to be safe in interactions with others, through embracing one's own power and controlling one's own awareness and actions, and that is the basis for freedom. And she offers these suggestions from a position of compassion because she understands well how difficult it can be to change.

So read her words and understand that the practical and effective steps she describes are not only solid self-defense advice, but also a way to change yourself for the better, offered with love and compassion."

— SHIHAN MARIA VAN DESSEL, 6th Dan and Chief Instructor of Eizan Ryu Jiu Jitsu and 4th Dan, World Oyama Karate

"Shihan Michelle enlists her unique experience, knowledge, and insights to offer simple and practical tools to navigate this complicated modern world. *Beyond Self-Defense* is a must-read for anyone who has ever felt that twinge of fear and uncertainty while riding a subway car late at night, or trying to size up a stranger or even a would-be friend."

— GREG KOTIS, Tony Award–winning author, playwright, and lyricist

"A groundbreaking approach to personal protection that transcends traditional self-defense techniques. Drawing from her extensive experience, Shihan Michelle teaches readers how to not only protect themselves but also serve as protectors of their communities. Through practical real-world examples, *Beyond Self-Defense* provides readers with the tools to assess and mitigate threats, defuse violent situations, and act as a force for good. Whether you're a seasoned martial artist or a commuter looking to improve your personal safety, this book is an essential guide for anyone looking to be responsible about their personal safety."

—MIKE LESSER, New York City parole officer and
senior law enforcement professional

"Such accessible writing, with a lovely personal touch—very relatable examples and 'real life' possibilities. The concept of Self Offense, without offensiveness, is fresh and attainable. This book is, in itself, a kata."

—PRUDENCE GLASS, activist, social worker, writer,
and former series producer at PBS's *American Masters*

"In my professional experience in law enforcement, I have seen the positive impact of self-defense training in violent crime scenarios. In this book you will find stories that engage you and insights that will transform your everyday life. I fully endorse Michelle's book as a valuable training tool that offers practical, not just theoretical, advice for anyone eager to become more alert, aware, and self-protected."

—SIMA RADUT BURGESS, special investigation
unit officer and former Secret Service agent

"In *Beyond Self-Defense,* Shihan Michelle uses her lifetime of karate and movement analysis practices to offer nuanced and necessary approaches to preventing the conditions under which assault occurs. . . . I couldn't stop reading and I hope every young person—every person—I know will read it too!"

—AYNSLEY VANDENBROUCKE LABAN, certified
movement analyst, and core faculty at Princeton
University program in dance

"Instead of playing defense, play offense. This book will teach you everything you need to know about taking the initiative and winning the day."

—SILENN THOMAS, producer of *300* and *The Spiderwick Chronicles*

BEYOND SELF-DEFENSE

How to Say No, Set Boundaries, and Reclaim Your Agency

SHIHAN MICHELLE, CMA
Creator of Self Offense

North Atlantic Books
Huichin, unceded Ohlone land
Berkeley, California

Published by
North Atlantic Books
Huichin, unceded Ohlone land
Berkeley, California

Cover design by Jess Morphew
Book design by Happenstance Type-O-Rama

Printed in the United States of America

Beyond Self-Defense: How to Say No, Set Boundaries, and Reclaim Your Agency is sponsored and published by North Atlantic Books, an educational nonprofit based in the unceded Ohlone land Huichin (Berkeley, CA) that collaborates with partners to develop cross-cultural perspectives; nurture holistic views of art, science, the humanities, and healing; and seed personal and global transformation by publishing work on the relationship of body, spirit, and nature.

North Atlantic Books's publications are distributed to the US trade and internationally by Penguin Random House Publisher Services. For further information, visit our website at www.northatlanticbooks.com.

CONTENT DISCLAIMER: This book contains material that may be triggering, including references to self-harm, sexual abuse, or trauma.

Library of Congress Cataloging-in-Publication Data

Names: Michelle, Shihan, author.
Title: Beyond self-defense : how to say no, set boundaries, and reclaim your agency / Shihan Michelle, CMA.
Description: Berkeley, CA : North Atlantic Books, [2024] | Includes bibliographical references and index. | Summary: "A feminist-forward guide to setting boundaries, assessing safety, and defusing violence using the self offense strategy"—Provided by publisher.
Identifiers: LCCN 2023039555 (print) | LCCN 2023039556 (ebook) | ISBN 9781623179984 (trade paperback) | ISBN 9781623179991 (ebook)
Subjects: LCSH: Women—Crimes against—Prevention. | Sex crimes—Prevention. | Sexual harassment of women—Prevention. | Self-defense for women. | Self-protective behavior.
Classification: LCC HV6250.4.W65 M4955 2024 (print) | LCC HV6250.4.W65 (ebook) | DDC 362.88082—dc23/eng/20231113
LC record available at https://lccn.loc.gov/2023039555
LC ebook record available at https://lccn.loc.gov/2023039556

1 2 3 4 5 6 7 8 9 VERSA 28 27 26 25 24

For Zelda—my daughter and hero. Thank you for your work on this book.

For all those who have been impacted by sexual violence and who have mustered or will muster the courage to share, to confront that happening, to own it and come out of the shadows—living your best life, free from the poison of resentment and regret, may well be your best revenge.

For all the men who got my "no" and especially those with whom I had the pleasure of changing my mind.

CONTENTS

PREFACE

The term sexual assault means any nonconsensual sexual act proscribed by federal, tribal, or state law, including when the victim lacks the capacity to consent.

It was the winter of 1977, and Lynn and Debbie wanted to party. Lynn's parents were out of town and had left fifteen-year-old Lynn and her older brother on their own. Their small Canadian town had few options for teenagers to socialize outside school in the middle of winter. They debated going to the mall or the ski club, but settled on the local hockey rink.

They convinced Lynn's brother to drop them off and assured him they would find their way home at the end of the evening. Before going in, they slipped around the side of the building to blow a joint. That's when they first caught sight of the two hot, slightly older guys who would forever change their lives. Giggling to themselves, they plotted how they could meet them.

At the end of the night, those same two guys offered Lynn and Debbie a ride home, and they accepted. The next day the police found Lynn in the back of a car parked in a driveway where she had been left, bruised and beaten, after being sexually assaulted, while her attacker, one of those guys, slept soundly inside his house. His roommate had called the cops. Go figure.

Lynn survived, as many do, and life went on. Lynn moved forward, fighting profound shame and rage, working hard not to let it consume her, burying her feelings, and making the best of it all.

She grew up, went to college, got married, had kids, and worked her butt off to be successful in every area of her life. She is successful. And she has lived her life in the shadow of that event.

Her parents never forgave themselves for leaving Lynn and her brother alone that weekend, and her brother blames himself for not having arranged to pick Lynn up at the end of the night. Like so many families impacted by sexual assault, they were deeply shaken in the wake of the pain and terror Lynn had experienced.

I'll never forget learning the news. My mother spoke to me in the way that mothers do when something terrible has happened to someone else's kid, and they want to rush to hug their own; I discovered this for myself as I raised my own children. I hung up the phone vowing to myself that I would never let that happen to me. I would never be so naive, careless, and stupid. I would be smarter; I would know better; I would see it coming. Except that I wasn't, I wouldn't, and I didn't.

The story of Lynn is based on the story of someone close to my family, and she could just as easily be a member of your family or someone you know. She could even be you. If you are someone who has already had an experience of being sexually assaulted, I have a specific request for you before you go any further with this book.

It won't work for you to use this book to blame yourself, beat yourself up, or take what I would call a "shoulda, woulda, coulda" approach. This book is not a referendum on why you were assaulted or a judgment of how it happened or why it shouldn't have happened. This book is not the truth about assault, or safety, or protecting yourself. It is also not a book for you to use to compare and belittle yourself or demean your choices.

Instead, it offers tools you can use to carve a powerful path forward for yourself, embracing your experience and circumstances in ways that empower, embolden, and inspire you. And it is, potentially, a powerful new perspective.

I invite you to consider that whatever you did or didn't do, said or didn't say, thought or didn't think, felt or didn't feel in that situation was exactly what was available to you in that situation. And anyone else with your set of circumstances in that situation would have done the same thing. You can't change what happened. You can resist it, avoid it, blame it, judge it, assess it, resent it, heal from it—and while all of this is completely valid, it still won't change what happened. However, you can move forward and past that experience. You can use the tools in this book to take action, to build on, to share, and even to recontextualize your experience. I humbly ask to be your partner in that journey.

And this book is not just for those who have experienced sexual assault. This book is also for those of you who have experienced harassment, belittlement, or bullying at work, at school, on the street, or even at home in your intimate relationships. And for those of you who experience fear or uncertainty when meeting new people, dating, traveling, or entering new relationships—from serious partnerships to casual hookups and everything in between. The tools in this book will empower you to make confident choices with anyone, anywhere, and at any time.

Over the years, I have had my own experiences navigating the world of taking risks, staying safe, and avoiding harm while dating, meeting new people, and hooking up. Starting at the age of fifteen, I had a lot of sex and did a lot of drugs and rock and roll. It was the late 1970s and early 1980s, and the real threat of AIDS was still years away. There were so many instances of saying yes to sex because it was easier than saying no.

One night, rather than going home, I accepted an offer to crash on a friend of a friend's couch only to wake up with my host naked and between my legs. My shout of surprise and reflexive push to get him off me were enough for him to stop. And if you had said to either one of us at that time that what had happened was sexual assault, we both likely would have balked. It was a misunderstanding, an accident, even; certainly not assault. We were naive, and the event seemed so banal, so ordinary—in other words, no big deal. He stopped. He apologized. No harm, no foul.

I met my husband when I was twenty-five and moved to New York City. We got married and started a family. I assumed that being married meant that because dating was behind me, so was the risk of being sexually harassed or assaulted. But no. I was a dancer and an actor. I was in New York City. I was going to be a star! There I was, standing in front of a casting director seated behind his desk in his office. I was wearing a thigh-length pencil skirt and high heels. I looked sophisticated and beautiful. He asked me to raise my skirt so he could see more of my legs. I thought to myself, *That's odd,* and I pulled my skirt up a few inches. Without taking his eyes off my legs, he held out his hand, palm side up, making a gesture that I took to mean "higher," and I lifted my skirt a bit more. I was hesitant—but kept following his direction. He repeated the gesture a third time, and my skirt inched higher until my panties were clearly visible. I was embarrassed, and felt awkward, and had a series of thoughts in a flash: *This is not right; I shouldn't have to do this,* quickly followed by *Maybe it's not such a big deal; it's not like he's touching me,* and *If I go along with this, he'll submit me for work* (he did). I wasn't harmed, but I did have to confront and make peace with having gone along with it. I could have walked out, and I didn't. I wanted something, and from my perspective, he had the power to grant what I wanted.

I know that I am drifting into tricky territory here. You might be thinking, *That's not fair; it wasn't her fault; he abused his power.*

Or you could be thinking, *How could she have been so stupid or weak to let him take advantage of her in that way?* Or how about, *No one should have to deal with that in the first place.* All understandable points of view, for sure. The problem is that not one of them leaves *me* with power. In both cases I am a victim—either a victim of the casting director or a victim of my own inability to stand up for myself. I prefer not to see it that way.

Rather than shaming or blaming myself or others, I work to own my actions by taking responsibility for them. And I am inviting you to do the same whenever possible. Because when Spidey's Uncle Ben says, "With great power comes great responsibility," the reverse, "With great responsibility comes great power," also holds true. When I talk about power, I mean the ability to take new actions in areas where we have been stuck or have experienced resignation, cynicism, or despair. Whenever we can own our actions and experiences and the impact, we have an opportunity to learn, and we get to be powerful in the face of what life throws at us. And the people around us get to experience that too.

In other words, as long as our experience remains one of being a victim of circumstance, blaming others and life for the ills that befall us, even when it is valid to do that, we do so at the risk of sacrificing real power and prolonging our suffering. This is not in any way, shape, or form meant to condone acts of violence or harassment, or absolve the people who commit them—not by a long shot. If we use my experience in the casting director's office as an example, it would be easy for me to stick myself with the following judgments: *He shouldn't have asked me to raise my skirt. That is an abuse of power. He was a creep.* Or for me to blame myself for being foolish, naive, or weak-minded. While those are valid reactions, they leave me and my world smaller. To use an exaggerated example: If someone has a horrible experience in a parking lot and as a result decides that the best way to keep that thing from happening again is never to use parking lots, their experience of life is without parking lots and therefore smaller. Suppose they then have a bad experience on a bus, and they choose to handle it the same way: no more bus rides. Now they can't ride a bus or go into parking lots, and their world is smaller still. They are now reducing the inherent risk that life is by reducing their travel options. Now, that doesn't mean that one shouldn't have their experiences in parking lots or on bus rides shine a light on future actions. But there is a big difference in including one's experience in future decisions: factoring it in as a possibility and taking appropriate precautions, and eliminating it from life altogether. In my case, it would sound like "I will never let myself be alone with a casting director; I will never wear a pencil skirt again; I will never trust another authority figure or man." I might even question whether I'm on the right career path and give up. When I am stuck being victimized by circumstances, my best options are to try to avoid or control those circumstances in the future, and living life that way raises the questions: How's that going? or, What is your experience of yourself and your life when you're living that way?

When I try to control or avoid past circumstances, I limit my options and my self-expression. My experience of myself is that I am small and fearful. Instead, I look at what actions I took or did not take and what had me take or not take those actions, and then my experience of myself is that I am bigger, and wiser, even. I am left contributed to by my experience and therefore have a new view to shine a light on my future choices. Experience, good or bad, has the potential to provide a new view or even wisdom. In this case, the action I took was to comply with his request to lift my skirt, because I reasoned that I wanted the job, and I needed to do this to get it. With the upbringing, education, and experience

I had, and without judgment, I say that was the best I could do in the moment. When I look from there, I can recontextualize the experience for myself from one who is at the effect of that experience to one who took the actions that had the experience go that way. And I can do that with compassion and a little admiration for the courage that it took for me to take that risk for what I was passionate about, even in the face of my inexperience. Owning that experience empowers me to keep going, to take new actions, and to stay open to possibilities. I am now bigger for my experience, not smaller.

Of course, this interpretation of victimhood or power is not the truth either. It's a creation—one that leaves me bigger for myself and with access to forgiveness and wisdom, and an openness to sharing my experience with others. It works for me. It leaves me with a say in my life.

I have been sexually assaulted, harassed, dishonored, disrespected, and, at times, compliant rather than consenting. I have also been lucky. And I acknowledge my white, cis, straight, able-bodied, middle-class privilege and how that has contributed to my being lucky. I am here to be of service—not tell you how it is for you. In the same way that there is no one way to go through life, there is no one way to stay safe and no one way to use this book. Some of it will make sense; you will agree with it, and you'll be willing to try it. Some of it, you may already be doing. Some of it may not work for you. Just because it's good information doesn't mean it's good for you. My goal is to give you tools to speak and act with power in the face of uncertainty, pain, harm, doubt, and fear—to help you live. No matter what, you can live with peace and purpose even when it seems impossible to do so. Take what you need and leave the rest.

■ ■ ■

In 1997, I applied for and was accepted into the St. Vincent's Rape Crisis Program. I was on call two or three times a month at St. Vincent's Hospital in Greenwich Village and the New York–Presbyterian Hospital in Lower Manhattan to advocate for survivors of sexual assault. A rape crisis advocate is the one person in the hospital whose sole reason for being there is to empower the survivor of a sexual assault. As an advocate, you are there, at the survivor's request, to be their support as they interact with doctors, nurses, family members, police, and the special victims unit. You are there as the survivor navigates the barrage of testing and as they consider whether to take prophylactic measures against pregnancy, HIV, and sexually transmitted disease infection. You are there as they try to make sense of—or, in some cases, try to recall—the events that led up to the assault. You are there as they endure the metaphorical probing into their life and actions and the literal probing of a rape kit. And you are there to witness and hold a space of compassion as they begin the journey of recovery. I volunteered in this capacity for a little over five years. It was at times scary, sad, enraging, humbling, and inspiring. It was always an honor.

During that time, I learned two things that surprised me. The first was that cis men get sexually assaulted. I had, up to that point, thought that sexual assault was a women's problem—but while women, both trans and cis, have certainly borne the lion's share of the burden, it isn't limited to women. Sexual assault is not a gender-specific problem.

The second thing I learned was that there is almost always some period of time where the person who attacks and the person who experiences the attack get to know each other. According to statistics from the Rape, Abuse & Incest National Network (RAINN), 80 percent of those who experience sexual assault report having known their attacker.* Getting to know each other can be as brief as was the case for one of the survivors I worked with, who accepted a ride home from a man she had just met, who said he was an off-duty police officer. Or it can be as long as many years, as was the case for another survivor, whose close male friend assaulted her in her apartment.

This shocked me. I had always imagined that if I were to be attacked it would be by a stranger coming up behind me in a dark alley or breaking into my home at night while I slept. We are taught to believe that sexual assault is perpetrated by fundamentally evil or sick people who lurk in shadows. This thinking blurs the fact that sexual assault is pervasive in our world and frequently occurs under what can only be characterized as ordinary and common-place circumstances. As you will discover in this book, the ingredients for sexual assault are already present in the background of many of our normal everyday interactions.

Around this time, I read a book titled *The Gift of Fear: And Other Survival Signals That Protect Us from Violence* by Gavin de Becker, a leading violence prediction and prevention expert. The book lays out the fundamental aspects of the conversations that generally precede an attack. It examines seemingly random acts of violence to help the reader predict and avoid finding themselves in dangerous situations. What struck me about the manipulations that de Becker's perpetrators used was how ordinary and subtle they were. And I wondered how I could bring these lessons to people in a way that would be relevant, personal, and, most importantly, actionable. In other words, move it from an informational model to an experiential one.

---

* RAINN, "Perpetrators of Sexual Violence: Statistics," www.rainn.org
/statistics/perpetrators-sexual-violence.

The final piece came as I completed a master's-level certification in Laban Movement Analysis—a comprehensive system for describing, visualizing, interpreting, executing, and documenting all varieties of movement, human and otherwise, and became a Certified Movement Analyst (CMA). I saw the opportunity to combine this expertise in movement analysis with my training as a martial artist and a rape crisis advocate, and I created a series of workshops— Self Offense, De-escalation and Listening, an antibullying program called Kids on the Offense, and an anti–sexual harassment training called Self Offense in the Workplace—that take a three-pronged approach to protecting oneself. I call these three prongs the Interview, which focuses on communication skills; the Dance, which emphasizes nonverbal movement factors; and the Getaway, a collection of release-and-run self-defense skills.

In this book you will find the practices for verbal and non-verbal boundary-setting from the Interview and the Dance, but nothing on the Getaway, which is beyond the scope of this book. The Getaway portion of our workshop is the smallest portion, for a few reasons. It is highly unlikely that you will be able to defend yourself with any certainty after a one-off workshop. For this reason we focus on and practice simple, easy-to-learn release-and-run self-defense principles and techniques. They are not included here, as I don't recommend that you learn self-defense from a book. It's a physical skill that requires in-person and consistent ongoing instruction and practice. I highly recommend that you get to experience the exhilaration and power that comes with learning how to break away from something as simple and scary as having your wrist grabbed, or escaping a grab from behind, or overcoming being knocked to the floor. Experience it in person and often. It is good practice that develops mental resilience, problem-solving under pressure, physical strength, flexibility, and stamina. And it's fun! If that calls to you, find yourself a reputable martial arts school or self-defense course. In fact, any kind of ongoing movement or athletic training that enlivens you and develops your coordination, strength, balance, timing, and ability to respond in the moment will likely increase your confidence, enjoyment, and resilience in everyday life, as well as your ability to respond to potential danger.

Over the years, people have shared with my team the difference that taking our workshop has made in their lives. Many of them leave the workshop with a new perspective that empowers them to set boundaries and advocate for themselves. They walk away with verbal and nonverbal awareness training and a methodology for spotting trouble with plenty of time for them to avoid having to fight their way out.

The aim of our work at Self Offense is to end sexual assault and harassment. We add our voices to those of the many individuals and organizations who stand for that outcome. However, we are creating a distinct context to fuel our actions. We are discarding the well-worn and oversimplified context of "good" victims and "bad" perpetrators, and introducing a model of accountability and ownership. It is a model where people can be held to account and hold others to account for harm caused, and where people can own the actions that they take or don't take, as well as the outcome of those actions.

As a result, I won't relate to anyone as a "victim" of sexual harassment or violence. But while I won't relate to them as victims, I am certainly not saying that what happened wasn't harmful or that they wanted it, asked for it, could have or should have avoided it, or that it was, in any way, shape, or form, their fault. I am out for people to have power, and as long as one remains victimized by an experience, there is a loss of power. I have enormous respect and compassion for what it takes to heal from a traumatic event. It often requires everything we have, applied more than once and over time, and we can easily backslide, stumble, and get stuck along the way.

At the same time, I am not here to vilify those who have caused harm. One of the things we invite people to recognize in our workshops is our own harm-causing nature—our own humanity. Without owning and taking responsibility for that, and then bringing radical compassion to our own ability to cause harm—accidentally or otherwise—how will we ever teach people to recognize their own harmful behavior and to correct it? And secondly, how will we ever forgive?

There is that word, *forgiveness.* Consider that forgiveness is something that you do for yourself first. Forgiveness is not letting someone off the hook or condoning behavior that caused harm. It is your willingness to stop drinking poison hoping that someone else will die, and in some cases hoping you will die if who you are unwilling to forgive is you. It is courageous, generous, and completely optional, and it has the potential to set you free.

I am standing for a new world of personal accountability, radical compassion, and ownership. In this world we can include all our history and experience; we can include feelings of pain, shame, anger, and resignation, and thoughts of revenge and regret. We can include them and not be limited by them. It will require radical compassion for the carelessness, arrogance, stupidity, and selfishness of others and for ourselves. It's a journey, a process of discovery, and even if we don't yet know what it will look like or what it will entail, I invite you to join me.

INTRODUCTION

Welcome to Self Offense.

Most attacks begin with a conversation, but not all conversations lead to an attack. How do you determine which ones will and which ones won't with plenty of time to keep yourself from having to fight your way to safety?

I am a 6th degree black belt and six-time women's full-contact karate champion, and even I don't want to have to fight my way to safety. A fight, even one you win, will cost you something—real injuries to your body, and likely longer-lasting injuries to your soul.

I suspect you would rather not have to fight your way out either, or you would have picked up a different book. I suspect you want to empower yourself to be safe, respected, and honored in your relationships—the short ones and the long ones. I suspect you want to live your life fully, freely, powerfully, and consensually. Truthfully, no matter how many YouTube videos you watch about how to kick a guy in the groin, shove your fingers in his eyeballs, and then bash your knee to his face, when confronted with the reality of it, you will probably freeze, freak out, or have your pepper spray taken away and sprayed back in your own eyes. Why? Because coming to your own rescue takes practice. You will find yourself alone with someone bigger than you, possibly drunk or high, attempting to extricate yourself from the situation or giving up, because, let's face it, often it's easier to just go along.

And you will likely survive it—God knows many people have and will. According to the Rape, Abuse & Incest National Network (RAINN), every seventy-three seconds, someone is sexually assaulted in the United States alone. Nine out of ten of those assaulted are women. One in six women will experience an attempted or completed rape, as will one in thirty-three men.* According to the National Center for Transgender Equality's 2015 U.S. Transgender Survey Report, one in two transgender people will experience sexual assault in their lifetime. In other words, half of all trans people![†] Through this book, I invite you to take a walk with me—a kind of heroic journey, with you as the hero. I am going to share some stories with you and offer some new perspectives and some recommended practices. The practices are simple, and some may even be familiar. This book will likely confirm and validate what you have already discovered works for you, it will add new practices and actions for you to take, and you may even find that it allows you to responsibly relax in areas where you have been hypervigilant, unsure, or afraid. You can expect to discover an elevated sense of confidence and peace of mind.

Self-Defense or Self Offense?

In the United States there exists a growing multibillion-dollar industry devoted to self-defense. One consistent message, particularly for women, revolves around situational scenarios advising

---

* RAINN, "Victims of Sexual Violence: Statistics," www.rainn.org/statistics /victims-sexual-violence.

† National Resource Center on Domestic Violence, "Violence against Trans and Non-Binary People," 2021, https://vawnet.org/sc/serving-trans-and -non-binary-survivors-domestic-and-sexual-violence/violence-against -trans-and.

them to be stronger, more aggressive, and dominating fighters without addressing the real challenge that successful fighting takes practice—thoughtful, dedicated, years-long practice—and a willingness to inflict gruesome harm on another. This industry perpetuates a victim-perpetrator binary, warning us against the bad people or perpetrators "out there" that we good people or potential victims need to protect ourselves from. However, they never seem to address the question: If we have to fight our way out of a situation, isn't it already too late?

Unless you plan to become proficient in tactical fighting or study for three to five years to become a black belt (and I am not saying you shouldn't do that—nothing would make me happier than to see the world populated by trained martial artists), you need Self Offense. Self Offense is a state change in personal protection that shifts us from reaction to proaction. It offers a way of thinking that empowers you to make smart and informed decisions about who, what, when, and where to trust. It is protective actions and techniques that you can put into practice immediately—you don't have to wait until it's an emergency.

This book addresses the period of time prior to an attack when we have the best shot of avoiding a physical altercation altogether. This is the essence of Self Offense. It will also take practice, but it is the kind of practice that best utilizes and leverages your natural senses and your own unique approach to living your life. It will help you expand your options and your ability to be present and empowered as you navigate a complex and nuanced world of relationships with friends, family, acquaintances, new people, and potential romantic partners. It will be immediately useful and relevant to your everyday life. It will not be scenario-driven; I will not be giving you "what to do if this specific thing happens" advice. I will be giving you a place from which to think and make decisions, and encouraging you to own the decisions that you make. Unlike self-defense tactics, Self Offense skills can be practiced anywhere, anytime, and with anyone. As I mentioned in the preface, there are three prongs to Self Offense: the Interview, the Dance, and the Getaway. In this book, we'll focus on the Interview and the Dance.

In the end, you are the expert in whatever moment you find yourself. Let me say that again: *You are the expert in whatever moment you find yourself.* You already have everything that you need to rescue yourself, if rescuing is what is required, and the more you practice the principles in this book, the more masterful you will become in living your best life safely, respectfully, and honorably.

Self Offense and your personal protection practice will move you from being aware and knowledgeable about how to be safe in the world to being someone who takes actions on a regular basis and is seen by others as someone who takes actions to be aware and stay safe. In other words, these practices will reduce the chances of your being targeted in the first place. Not because you read about it—because you took the action!

It's time to unleash your inner hero.

Self Offense Becomes Second Nature

Many of us are taught growing up—and some of us learn later in life, a.k.a. the hard way—that boundary-setting is a key component of managing relationships and situations in life. In Self Offense we inquire into how boundary-setting or the absence of it directly impacts our ability to feel and be safe and powerful in the world. Self Offense begins with the natural and deliberate actions that you take or don't take to keep yourself safe and set those boundaries. Some of these actions or behaviors may be obvious, and you might already be doing some of them, and some will be discoveries that we will make together along the way—brand new practices that you can begin using and repeat until they become natural.

For example, you likely already have things you do, actions you take, when you are walking by yourself and you get a feeling that something is off; when you suspect that someone is following you or a stranger calls out "Hey, baby!" Maybe you pull out your phone and call a friend, or you keep walking, only a little faster, while furtively glancing in shop windows to see if they are still there—or maybe you turn around and flip them the finger. Whatever it is, it's your way of handling it. It works for you, and we don't want to mess with what works. We do want to bring ownership to these actions—more on that later. What makes us able to handle a stressful situation naturally and without appearing to try is the degree of practice or training that we have available to draw on. In Self Offense, we start with what you are already good at—the actions you are already taking to protect yourself or to establish and maintain your boundaries. You may describe it as "common sense" or "what my parents taught me" or "what works for me" or "how I know myself in any given situation." This is where Self Offense begins, and we expand and practice from there.

When you stop and think about it, the idea that you and I will know how to handle a potentially life-threatening situation without any training or practice is aspirational at best. As a professional martial artist, I know that it takes years of dedicated consistent practice to respond effectively to a physical threat versus reacting impulsively.

One of the most compelling aspects of training in the martial arts is that it reveals not only our physical strengths and weaknesses but our emotional, mental, and spiritual ones as well. The major structure provided to develop mastery and discipline in traditional Japanese martial arts is called *kata,* which means "way of doing." A kata is a formal exercise; each kata follows a fixed series of steps: precise arm movements, steps, kicks, and so forth, with emphasis on the exact form of each movement and its order. You have probably seen videos of people practicing these sets of movements. The goal of kata is to provide a structure for practicing the most basic and complex forms and processes that constitute mastery in any given arena. Mastery is present when the principles of kata arise organically, appropriately, reliably, and spontaneously in real-life situations. In other words, they become second nature. The thing is, you can't achieve mastery without practice, and when you stop practicing, you can certainly expect a diminishment, right up to the disappearance of mastery. You can't have one without the other.

To help you gain mastery in Self Offense, I have created eight kata for you to practice under ordinary and relaxed circumstances. These kata are designed to train you to be proactive in protecting yourself so that you can recognize potential danger with plenty of time to keep yourself from ever having to fight your way out of a situation. And do so in a way that is graceful, powerful, and completely consistent with how you want to be living your life.

There are a number of journal prompts and reflection opportunities throughout this book. You may wish to keep a notebook or journal nearby as you're going through the book to record your thoughts and responses to these prompts. I highly recommend that you use them. This will assist you in grounding the work in your life.

REFLECTION

- What actions do you already take to protect yourself?

- What preventative actions do you take when you travel?

- What preventative actions do you take when you use public transportation or enter and exit public parking lots and garages?

- What preventative actions do you take when going on a first or second date?

- What preventative actions do you take when heading out to a concert or bar with friends?

- What preventative actions do you take when getting into a rideshare or taxi?

1

The Power of Context

The following is a story summarized from Gavin de Becker's *The Gift of Fear*. We use this scenario in our workshop as a jumping-off point for the conversations on Self Offense. The first conversation is that of context.

> A young woman enters her apartment building, laden with grocery bags. She notices that the front door to her building has been left ajar. She enters the building and begins climbing the stairs to her apartment. Halfway there, a bag breaks, and a cat food can spills out, clattering down the stairs.
>
> From the stairwell below she hears a friendly voice. "Got it! I'll bring it up." She looks down and sees a handsome, well-dressed man with a warm smile. He holds up the stray can, and then looks down at the bags she's holding. "Oh, let me give you a hand."
>
> Kelly smiles. "No, no, thanks. I've got it."
>
> The man holds his hands out to take the groceries. "You don't look like you've got it. What floor are you going to?"
>
> Kelly lowers her eyes shyly and says, "The fourth, but I'm okay, really."

The man insists, "I'm going to the fourth floor too and I'm late—not my fault, broken watch—so let's not just stand here. And give me that!"

He reaches out to grab hold of the bags. They are now both holding the bags, and in another attempt to shake off this helpful stranger Kelly protests, saying kindly, "No, really! Thanks, but, no, I've got it."

The man then looks directly at Kelly and says seriously, "There's such a thing as being too proud, you know." There is a brief pause as Kelly lets go of the bags. The man swings into action. "We better hurry," he says excitedly. "Did you know a cat can live for three weeks without eating? I'll tell you how I learned that little tidbit. I once forgot that I had promised to feed a cat while a friend of mine was out of town."

They soon arrive in front of Kelly's door, and she turns to face him and says, "I'll take it from here."

He protests, "Oh, no. I'm not going to let you have another cat food spill. We can leave the door open like ladies do in old movies. I'll just put the bags down and go."

Kelly hesitates, looks at her door, and then looks back to this friendly, helpful, handsome stranger. He smiles and says sincerely, "I promise."

Kelly smiles, sighs, and opens the door. The man quickly moves past her and disappears into the apartment. Kelly lingers at the door and places a bag of groceries against the door to hold it open. She turns to glance around the hallway and down to the stairwell before disappearing into the apartment. In the next moment, the man returns to the doorway and picks up the bag of groceries holding open the door. He too glances briefly into the hallway before retreating into the apartment, closing the door behind him.

What happens next? In your journal, write down the first thing that comes to mind.

If you wrote "She gets assaulted," or "He attacks her," or even just "Nothing good," it is very likely that what influenced your answer was the fact that you are reading a personal protection handbook. From the moment you began reading the scenario, you were likely waiting for something bad to happen. It's likely you were unknowingly assuming something bad would happen— or actively looking for it. After all, you are not an idiot! Why else would we present the scenario in a personal safety handbook?

Now imagine you're reading the same scenario in a book titled *101 Ways to Meet the Person of Your Dreams.*

Imagine yourself in a bookstore. You are single, ready to meet someone new. The actions you have taken, so far, haven't resulted in you meeting the person of your dreams. You spot a book that promises new opportunities and new openings for action around love and romance. You open it and start reading a meet-cute scenario where two strangers happen to meet on the stairs. The woman is struggling with too many grocery bags, and one of them breaks open, spilling a can of cat food down the stairs. She turns around and, as if out of thin air, a charming and handsome man comes to her rescue and catches the can. As he hands it to her, their eyes meet, and he offers to help her carry those heavy bags the rest of the way to her apartment. After hesitating, she accepts, and they end up in her apartment.

Now ask yourself the same question: What happens next? Write down whatever comes to mind.

Is it possible that you have a different answer from what you thought earlier? Very likely it is. Even if you remain suspicious, it will be in the context of meeting the person of your dreams: "The person of my dreams would never try to hurt me or take advantage of me."

You see, what often gets missed when we are assessing a situation is the context that is operating in the background, influencing our interpretations of events and circumstances. When the question "What happens next, after that scenario?" was initially posed, you likely didn't think to yourself, *I'm reading a personal protection handbook; therefore, I think she gets attacked*—at least, not until that idea was explicitly stated in the text. What is more likely is that you were expecting it all along, looking for it. Again, why else would we include the story?

Compare and contrast the same question "What happens next?" when the same scenario is encountered in the context of the love, romance, and relationships section of your local bookstore. You likely didn't stop to think, *Well, I am in the love, romance, and relationships section of the bookstore, so I bet they fall in love.* You were expecting that, looking for that, ultimately set up for that or something along the lines of a meet-cute story.

In both examples, what changes is the context and the correlated conclusion; the content remains the same. What context do you think generally drives your daily life? Do you live your life like you are a character in a murder mystery or a scary movie? Are you looking for something bad to happen around every corner, suspicious of everyone you meet? If you're someone who has already experienced harm—either growing up in a violent or abusive household, or having been bullied or ostracized at school or in your community—it would make perfect sense that you would be living like you're a character in a suspense movie, and it may well be what propelled you to pick up this book.

Or are you more likely to give the benefit of the doubt to people while looking for things to work out happily? You like to view life with rose-colored glasses because your life has been pretty charmed so far—no reason why it shouldn't continue that way, especially if you are talking to someone who looks like they belong in your romantic comedy or love story. Or if they just seem really nice, helpful, or nonthreatening. You very likely fall somewhere in between, where it depends on the circumstances or environment, or how you are feeling at any given moment. But it is also heavily influenced by the context that is shaping how that moment is occurring for you. For example, when it is nighttime, you may be more on guard or suspicious than you are during the daytime, if how nighttime occurs for you is that it is a more dangerous time. That it occurs as more dangerous is shaping how you view what happens at night, and the conclusions you draw, and the actions you take. Someone walking behind you during the day will likely occur differently, less threatening, than at night simply because of the shift in how life occurs seen through the lens of dangerous night.

I was recently rewatching the 1989 movie *Shirley Valentine* and was struck by the scene between Shirley and the Greek restaurant owner Costas Dimitriades. After Shirley has dinner by herself in his restaurant, they meet and get to chatting, and he walks her back to her hotel. He invites her to spend the next day on his boat. She says no several times, and he persists. He says, "You are afraid. You are afraid that I will make [sex] with you." He is charming, he is sincere, and he is kind. She denies being afraid. He goes on to explain his good intentions, promises to be honorable, and eventually wins her over. Their date for the next day is set. He is true to his word and treats her with honor and respect, and they eventually have consensual sex with each other. At no point during this exchange did I think to myself, *Beware, Shirley. Your boundaries aren't being honored! He could be a dangerous man.* It's a romantic comedy, and that becomes the subtle yet decisive context for my interpretation.

I'm not pointing this out because you shouldn't be having context or circumstances shape your view, but you want to be able to notice that you are thinking and acting from a particular context or circumstance. Once you notice the context that is shaping your view, it stops being in the background and becomes content that you can do something with—even if that is just acknowledging that it is strongly influencing your thinking and the actions you are taking or not taking. Ultimately, wouldn't it be better to have a context that gives you access to practicing judging where and when to let your guard down or raise it, that includes the circumstances you are already thinking, planning, and acting from but isn't limited by them? More on that later. Now, if you are someone who lives with the weight and accompanied exhaustion of living in a constant state of being hyperalert—suspicious or untrusting of everyone you meet, constantly scanning the environment for potential threats, startled by loud or sudden noises—practicing the tools in this book can bring some welcome relief and access to peace of mind. And if you are hypervigilant in this way, you very likely have had experiences in your past that shape this context for life and justify your caution.

However, hypervigilance can rob you of the kind of relaxed mind that responds best to sudden and unexpected circumstances. It can cause undue stress and lead you to miss opportunities due to overthinking and overreacting. It can become a kind of tunnel vision that has you avoiding all kinds of situations, social and otherwise, out of a concern or fear that you can't trust anyone and that you can't properly defend yourself if the need arises. What would your life be like if you could utilize that vigilance as a situation-specific tool rather than as a persistent state of mind?

What's Your Context?

We all occupy a variety of contexts in life, and those contexts or settings impact how we behave and the actions that we may or may not take in any given situation. For instance, it is normal for people to punch and kick each other in a karate dojo (school) but wildly inappropriate in a restaurant. It makes perfect sense for me to be crammed tight in a subway car at rush hour with strangers pressed close to me, but it would be super weird to find people so close in the changing room at the YMCA.

Context also operates in how we view ourselves in relationship to our status or power in any given interaction with another. I am an employee (low status) and they are a boss (high status), or I am a student (low status) and they are a teacher (high status), or we are friends (similar or equal status). It is not uncommon for there to be a status difference between men (seen as high status) and women (seen as low status) and other gender expressions (low status). These shifts in context will impact how we interact and what we consider appropriate or inappropriate in any given situation. To make things more complex, these contexts often include an imbalance of power that can easily render one person impotent to set boundaries and another person entitled to ignore boundaries that are set. For now, I invite you to begin to notice the contexts that are at play in your interactions with others and how they influence your actions.

Back to the original question: What happens next in Kelly's story?

On the surface, the conversation between Kelly and the man in the stairwell is about as normal and nonthreatening as a conversation could be. Check it out. Go back and read the scenario out loud to yourself. Read it without inflection or emotion. Notice that nothing said is inherently sinister. There is nothing that is said by either of them that you haven't said or had said to you at some point. While the content of the conversation might have been different, the nature of the conversation is superficial and

polite. Ask yourself how many superficial and polite conversations
you have had with perfect strangers.

   We think we're going to know it when we see it, but if you consider all the potential contexts at play—some of them conflicting—
you just might not. How to listen for potential danger and what to
do to create certainty and trust when there is suspicion or doubt
(and even when there isn't) is what we will be exploring in this
book and urging you to practice in your life. We will be looking at
how you interact, set boundaries, and stay or avoid being in control, and how those behaviors can impact your safety. In the next
chapter, I will give you a context that you can use, at a moment's
notice, to assess whether you are willing to trust a person or situation, and I'll give you the tools to take confident action.

REFLECTION AND PRACTICE

- Do you have, or have you had, colleagues at work that you
  also consider friends?

- Do you have, or have you had, teachers or bosses that you
  also consider friends?

These are two areas where roles can overlap; therefore, how
you behave in these relationships is not strictly professional or
strictly social. I work with my daughter, and we often have to deal
with our relationship in a fluid way. Sometimes we are parent-child,
sometimes teacher-student, sometimes business partners, and
sometimes friends. My name changes depending on the context.
At any given time on any given day, she will address me as Mom,
Shihan, or Michelle. And that alerts us to the context. On my end,
she is either Zelda, "Flower," or Sensei.

Practice identifying the various environmental contexts (home, school, work, a party) and relationship contexts or roles (friend, boss, sibling, student) that show up in your life and notice whether some contexts or roles empower you more than others.

Over the course of your day and throughout your week, make a list of the different situational contexts and roles that you play in your life (friend, lover, sibling, child, boss, coworker, employee, parent). Are there any roles or settings in which you feel your ability to act freely is constrained? Are there any in which you feel much more freedom to act?

2

No Way Know How

Saying no or setting a boundary is the single most powerful tool that I can offer you in your quest to live your life both empowered and safe.

When you say no or set some boundary with another person, you will discover important information about them. You will get to see how they deal with not getting what they want or being rejected—at least in that moment. This information, even on a small scale, can give you a powerful insight into the kind of person you are dealing with, and whether or not they are going to listen to you now or in the future. This then becomes a foundation for your choosing to trust this person or not. In Self Offense, we take this a step further and recommend that you say no proactively in order to determine whether the person you are interacting with is listening to you and accepting you setting a boundary. We will talk about this in even more detail later in the book. Think back to a time when you were getting to know someone and everything was going great. They seemed friendly, happy, and kind right up until you said no or disagreed with them about something. In an instant, it became a Jekyll-Hyde moment. They got upset or became mean or cold or dismissive.

You can learn a lot about someone in an instant when you say no or set a boundary with them, whether you are testing them for safety or not. It is useful in general and has the added benefit of being a safety practice. Even having a difference of opinion or voicing a different approach to handling a situation can elicit reactions that set off subtle alarms. Are they willing to listen to you and consider another way of doing something? Are they open to letting you lead the way? This can be a useful barometer in deciding whether to move forward in your interactions or relationships with people. I invite you to bring the "no" test to a variety of interactions—with coworkers, clients, romantic partners, friends, or acquaintances. The more you practice, the easier and more natural it will become.

There is one major problem with using "no" as a tool to find out who you are dealing with, and that is that most of us are not very good at it. In fact, I have yet to meet anyone who is confident saying no to anyone, anywhere, and at any time. If you see yourself as someone who is the exception, I respectfully invite you to consider that you may have a blind spot, or if you don't, it may be that the work for you to do lies in receiving and respecting the no's of others. You could also look to see if where you are comfortable saying no is when you know that "no" is the answer, when it is clear for you that you want to say no or you don't care that much about it, or when the stakes are low. I invite you to consider that there are likely areas where it is not as clear for you, and I invite you to stay open to the possibility that there are situations, relationships, and occasions in your life when it is not as clear-cut, and you may find it more difficult to say no.

The Politics of No

There are cultural expectations and roles assigned in society for cis men and women that impact the dynamics of "no." These are not intrinsic masculine or feminine traits. They are not the absolute truth regarding gender dynamics, and they are not mutually exclusive to cis men and women. However, these expectations and roles do reflect and impact the lived experience of many people and may provide some insight for you into your own relationship with no. In many cultures, cis women are often socialized to be accommodating and to resist conflict; they are told to make others feel at ease—"Make nice," "Get along," "Don't be difficult." They are the caregivers and are often told, explicitly or implicitly, that the needs of others should come before their own. Women need to be pleasing—otherwise it's unattractive, unbecoming, and, ultimately, not feminine. "Don't be a nasty woman." "She's a bitch."

On the flip side, in many cultures, cis men are encouraged to be persistent, and in some cases, aggressively persistent. "Boys will be boys." "Man up." "She's playing hard to get; she really wants it." "Don't be a pussy, wimp, pansy, or doormat." Men need to be seen as assertive and dominating—otherwise it's unattractive and weak. This binary is pervasive and goes beyond individual expressions of gender. It impacts many of our societal systems, from media representation and politics to the gender wage gap.

Additionally, much of American—and Western—culture and history glorify persistence and dominance. The United States as a country was built on the premise that a group of people—white Englishmen—knew better how to govern themselves in a "new" land and had the right to take whatever they needed, and from whoever, when they arrived. The ideas of independence and manifest destiny helped early American settlers, and those who came afterward, justify the domination of others for the greater good. But if one group of people felt it was okay to take, there was a group being taken from. Modern American culture has inherited this blend of mixed signals and conflicting values—seeking forgiveness and not permission, never taking no for an answer, and "taking the frontier" or laying claim to someone else's domain. It is no wonder that we find ourselves where we are today, with some people culturally disempowered from saying no, and others feeling justified in ignoring a boundary.

For much of American and Western society, the ideas of rape culture, consent, and historical oppression are new. But until we fundamentally deal with the conflict of who gets to say no and when (hint—it should be anyone, anytime), we are doomed to blame and shame individuals instead of identifying and solving some of the root issues in our culture.

Adding Nuance to No and Harm Prevention

The Me Too movement was started by activist Tarana Burke and gained well-deserved recognition and momentum in 2017. The movement focuses on those who survive and speak out against harassment and sexual assault using the hashtag #MeToo, and it has been an important cultural reckoning. People have fought for and reclaimed agency from the normalized systemic abuses of power and the tolerance of sexual violence across our society. At all levels, from the home to the executive office, we have to face the fact that American society (and many others) has systematically tolerated and even sanctioned the entitled and perverse actions of many of the leaders and power players in our industries and communities. The Me Too movement and what followed have been a ginormous win for those who have been harmed and silenced, and a win for future generations who will stand on our shoulders with new power to say no in the face of abusive behavior—to state "This will not be tolerated."

But with this zero-tolerance approach that some institutions, large and small, have been taking, there has been a quiet cost— the potential harm it can cause to the accused. This stance may be rejected or deemed controversial by those who have been hurt or had those close to them hurt by sexual violence or harassment. Yet, in the same way we're urged to address all sides of any complex issue, I'm asking that we set aside any immediate and valid indignation to consider the harm that can and will happen when people are falsely accused or threatened with public accusation or when we use words like *harassment, abuse, trauma,* or *assault* to describe any and all harm that people experience.

When we take a zero-tolerance stance and always believe the person who comes forward as a victim, we risk the pendulum swinging in the opposite direction. Because we have so grossly ignored the harm against (mostly) women and are now trying to right this wrong, some accusations, made in the right way to the right people, whether false or not, are treated as the truth. There is a caveat here, of course; those with more social power—white upper-class cis women, for example—are more likely to be believed compared to those with less social power. Still, in some circles, a taboo is forming. "Believe women" has turned into "Don't believe men," and this is a problem, especially for our young men, many of whom are also trying to navigate this new world that they, too, have inherited.

When people speak about false accusations of sexual violence or harassment, this usually implies that the person who made the accusation is intentionally lying, that they have an intent to cause harm. While this is not an impossibility, I am going to make a different assertion. When people make a "false accusation," one of two things has happened. Either they have been harmed in some way and are using the now-often-used terms *assault* or *harassment* to speak to an experience they had, without awareness or without care for the weight of those terms and what they could mean; or they have justified that "false accusation" because they think that the person they are accusing deserves to be punished in some way. Both of these scenarios are an abuse of power, even if an unintentional one, that we must begin to address, without stepping over the harm that caused the false accusation. We are fighting so hard for those that experience harm to be heard that we are tolerating an egregious generalized speaking that can cause irreparable harm.

One of my martial arts students who is in high school told me a story about her ex-boyfriend. He was accused by a girl in the school of having harassed her. When the girl brought this to her parents and subsequently the administration, she said that what happened to her was so traumatic that she couldn't say what exactly happened—but she was clear that she had been harassed. This young man was now accused of harassment, which he denied, but had no recourse to address what he actually did that she experienced as harassment. This spread throughout the school and that young man was labeled a "perpetrator." The damage was done; it didn't matter that no one could actually point to what he did that was harmful. He left the school. What choice did he have? This story is not to prove that false accusations happen or to justify not listening to those who are victimized, but it is a cautionary tale of what happens when we throw out our willingness to address the nuances of these situations in favor of "Believe all victims."

Self Offense is out to transform how we have conversations about harm and how we address harm when it happens to us and when it happens to others. Until we fundamentally shift our view from "Who's at fault?," "Who's to blame?," and "Who deserves our sympathy?" to inquiring into "What happened?"—asking what actions were taken, what words were spoken, and what context those actions took place in—we are doomed to continue to react to harm instead of prevent it.

Here is the thing: this is challenging. Most of us are not trained to speak from what is happening; we are trained to speak from our descriptions of what is happening. Think of watching a sporting event. The commentator has two kinds of speaking. One is the speaking that happens before and after the game, or in between plays, that is analytical and descriptive. It brings in a bigger context that includes the player, the team history, and so forth. Compare this with the speaking during the game or the play itself. This speaking details the actions of the game exactly as they are happening. It doesn't matter if you are actually seeing the game—you can see what is happening from what is being said by the commentator. Both ways of speaking are important and contribute to the overall experience of watching the game, and they are distinct.

Often, when we address issues of harm, they are addressed primarily in the descriptive, analytical, and conceptual realm, and exclusively in a victim-perpetrator binary. We then argue over whose description or analysis of what happened is the truth. We speak from a conclusion we have made about the events, instead of speaking from an inquiry into the event itself. People get relegated into categories of good-bad, right-wrong, or victim-perpetrator, and as a result we fundamentally objectify and whittle down all the nuance of what happened into a concept of what happened, and then make judgments from there. It is easy to be dismissive when people are seen only as objects; it is easy to justify a harsh punishment when what you are punishing is just a thing: a monster.

Analyzing and reviewing events is valid, but it's important to account for the whole story within a larger analysis. When we speak to what literally happened during an event, it will force us to create space between our initial judgments and our ability to address the actual event. When we can hold what is happening or what happened *and* our analysis of what happened with equal weight, we make room for all the nuance that addressing harm requires. This is the space in which education is possible, restorative justice is possible, people seeing and acting newly is possible because they don't have to get out from under a character analysis or judgment that has been added to their actions. No one is necessarily a bad person in their own narrative—not without justification. If we are really interested in making a difference and preventing harm from occurring, we have to be willing to bring compassion and ask ourselves what might it be like for someone who took a harmful action—before, during, and afterward. Only then can we address what had them perpetrate the harm and shift it so that it doesn't happen again.

We can't wait for the people we say are the wrongdoers to agree with our negative judgments of their character, and magically see it our way, and stop causing harm. No one is willing to look at how they can be better if what they are confronted with is "This is what is wrong with you; now change." As long as we are blaming and shaming people, there is no room for nuance, and it directly undermines our ability to heal the harm caused. Though we might want revenge for the harms that have been done to us— we want the bad guy to be punished, and we want them to feel the pain we have felt—it's ultimately more compassionate to address someone who has caused harm from a place of being willing to understand. This is how we prevent future harms, not just get revenge for older ones.

Self Offense is asking you to be willing to hold it all in your view—to bring all of your analysis and judgment with equal weight as your demand to know *exactly* what happened. A willingness to go beyond what is simple, what is black-and-white, and continue to make space. Nuance is challenging because it opens up inquiry, while analysis and conclusions close them. It is not as satisfying and often leaves us with more questions than answers, but it is the fundamental work of getting down in the dirt of addressing harm and preventing it. It is not simple. It is messy. But it is vital to our pursuit of preventing harm and healing harm caused.

When We Say No

Many of us may be able to say no if we are angry, offended, or upset. But it gets more complex when, for example, we want to say no to the someone from whom we are hoping to get a yes about something that we want: a paycheck, a ride home, their time and attention. We rationalize that we can't very well give a no for fear that we will get a no in return. Or, similarly, we want to say yes because we like them—and we're afraid that saying no will make them not like us.

On the flip side, most of us are also not very good at being told no without getting angry, upset, or offended—especially when we want something. Maybe we say to ourselves, *They must not understand how important this is to me.* Or, *I know what is best for everyone in this situation.*

You see, it's often easy to say no when you feel adamant about it and when you don't really care how the person responds, just as it's easy to accept no from another when the stakes are low or you don't care deeply about the issue. You might already be thinking of examples of when it was easy to say no. Like that time when that creep tried to buy you a drink or that loser wanted to take you out, or when you were going to quit the job anyway, and your boss asked you to stay late and work on a project, or when a telemarketer asked you to sign up for a new car warranty. But what about when the stakes are higher—like when you also want something from them? What about when they're really cute, and it seems like they're into you? What if you want the job and you're afraid that saying no will jeopardize your chances? Or what if you're afraid that turning down this invitation will mean you won't get another one in the future? This was the predicament that I found myself in the time I stood in front of a casting director hoping he would submit me for auditions as I awkwardly inched my skirt higher and higher at his request.

You may be beginning to see the nuance and complexity of saying no and setting boundaries in your own life. You may be beginning to see that, like most people, you have trouble saying no at least some of the time, in certain situations, or with certain people.

You may see yourself as a people-pleaser and be struggling to see how you can be any other way. I get it. Hang in there. This is why we call it a *practice*. Or you might be one of the rare individuals who never has a problem saying no. If so, great—and what will make a difference is to consider that there may be some places where you are not empowered to say no clearly, directly, or effectively. Or there may be circumstances where you aren't so great at receiving a no. Allow yourself to examine your life as you reflect and give yourself permission to expand and discover new ways to say no and to practice receiving no from others.

Saying no is an action that you can take once or many times in an interaction, and at any point in a relationship when you want to set a boundary or determine if another person's listening to and respecting your boundary-setting. For most of us, saying no or being contrary will happen during the natural course of most relationships. If you bring awareness to these occurrences, especially those in which you say no and the person is not listening or accepting it, that information alone can empower your next action.

Learning to Say No

What are the reasons that you have for not saying no when that feels like the best answer? These are some answers people often share with my team during our workshops. Circle or write down the ones that resonate for you.

- You are afraid that you will upset the person. Maybe you have had an experience where saying no has made the person angry or violent, and you don't want that to happen again.
- You are afraid that you will make the situation worse for yourself. There will be some retaliation or unfavorable impact either in the moment or down the road.
- You want something from them. You strategize that if you say no to them, they may say no to you.
- You don't want to hurt their feelings. *Consider that it is because you don't like how it feels for you to hurt their feelings.*
- You don't want to appear unkind, ungrateful, prejudiced, sexist, rude, uncaring, or just plain bad, mean, or wrong.

While these are all valid reasons, at the end of the day, I want to give you the opportunity to notice these reasons and to own them as your reasons, your logic, and your feelings, rather than as a judgment or declaration against the other person or situation so you can still take action. Whenever you say no to someone, you are not saying no to who they are as a person; you are saying no to what the person is requesting or asserting. This is also true for when someone says no to you.

Given that we are often not comfortable and confident to say no directly, there are other ways we have found to communicate no. What is it that you say or do to communicate that no without saying the word *no* directly?

- "Maybe?"
- "I'll think about it."
- "That's definitely an option."
- "Thanks anyway."
- "Let me check my calendar and get back to you."
- "I'm pretty sure that I am busy that day."
- "I'd like to, but . . ."

Come up with a reason or pretense for why you can't say yes—lies, reasons, and excuses can be good Self Offense. In fact, it can be good to have a few prepared ahead of time so you can say them with conviction.

My friend Richard has worked it out with his wife that if she ever has trouble leaving a conversation, she should say that she has to leave to help him with something. Perfect Self Offense! Here are some other ways to say no without directly using the word.

- Pretend you didn't hear or ignore them and say nothing, hoping they won't notice and will move on.
- Avert your gaze or blankly stare back as you say nothing. Remember all those times you didn't respond to a text.

- Change the subject. Again, hoping they won't notice or they will get the hint.
- Make a joke or deflect in some way. Surely, if you can make them laugh, they will leave you alone.

There is also a category of saying no where we actually say yes but with no real commitment to make the request happen. It might go something like this: You bump into an old friend or acquaintance on the street. After a brief catch-up, you say, "We should get together soon." They respond with, "Yes, we really should. I'll give you a call," and you say, "Great, I look forward to hearing from you." And as you are walking away, you think to yourself, *That's never going to happen.* This "non-no, no" is when you say "yes" out loud, but you say to yourself, *That call is never going to happen,* or *Wow, I just agreed to something I have no intention of following through on.* You might wind up ignoring the person's texts or calls, or not taking the initiative of following up with them. This type of no relies on inaction. "Ghosting" also falls under this category. Take note that this is the stickiest no of all because it often relies on the situational or relationship context or the tone of someone's speaking. If you say yes and you mean no, at some point, unless the offer or request is dropped, you will likely need to offer a more direct no.

On the flip side, when you hear a yes that seems to lack genuine authenticity, it might actually be a no. This also gets tricky because now we're interpreting tone and body language, which can be difficult for many of us. Notice whether they are not making eye contact with you, or appear to be unenthusiastic in tone, or start speaking softly or physically squirming or shifting. These are not rules of body language, but they can give you an indication that you may need to check in with them again and request a clearer yes or no. In these instances you might say something like, "Are you sure?," "Would you rather not?," or "It might not work for you to say yes or agree," and give them an opportunity to be clear or work out a counterproposal. I say this in particular for cis men who have been raised in a culture of persisting in the face of no. This may also serve to keep you from entering an interaction that you think is consensual, but you find out later that for them, it was not. This is one of the ways Self Offense can serve to keep you safe, even if you are less concerned with being forced into a situation. While it may seem obvious in the cold light of day, this type of interaction— one that started as consensual and then moved to something that one party sees as nonconsensual after the fact—is especially tricky when drugs or alcohol are in the mix. Being high or drunk makes it even more challenging for both parties to speak up and listen effectively. These are all factors to own whenever you are interacting with people to keep yourself and others safe and empowered.

At the end of the day, when it comes to your safety and the use of no and boundary-setting as a proactive tool, what you say to communicate no is not the most important thing. What is most important is that you know that you are saying no, and you do not let yourself get persuaded out of that no. If you do let yourself be persuaded, notice that, and own it as a choice. Even a kind, gentle, sweet "I'll think about it" or "maybe" will accomplish the task if you stick with it—keep saying whatever it is you are saying to communicate no. If you are saying "maybe," *keep saying "maybe."* If you are saying "I'll think about it," repeat that phrase until they get the point. *Persistence communicates.* Like the dripping water that cuts through the rock over time, persistence is effective. You'll notice that after offering the third or fourth "maybe" or "I'll think about it," it starts to get . . . weird. And if you find yourself thinking, *This is weird! I can't keep saying "maybe" forever,* I have a little exercise for you. Right now, say "maybe" ten different ways, using different inflections, different intentions, and different volumes; get creative. You really can do it. It just takes practice.

You may also find yourself getting annoyed, frustrated, or exasperated with having to repeat yourself, and this might be the very fuel you need to be more direct with your "no" communication. At the end of the day, whatever it is that you say or do to communicate your no, notice that you are clear that you mean no as you are saying or doing whatever you are saying or doing. Even in the face of a soft, indirect, or nonverbal no, consider that the person you are saying it to knows you are communicating a no. This is a powerful place to come from, if only for the purpose of fortifying your persistence with your no or to escalate or double down when you see fit.

Below are some examples of how persisting with no can be effectively used in a variety of different situations, thus determining the safest or best course of action in an interaction.

When the "No" Gives You All You Need to Know

Nancy's Story

I am a nurse, and I respond to 911 calls. A male coworker (it is important to mention that he was male only because he was much larger than me) said he had to show me something, but this would have taken me off a work task and put us in an environment where we were completely alone, in the middle of the night, outside. I told this coworker *no*. Flat out. No. He continued to insist that I pay attention to what he wanted to show me. I want to be clear that this was not sexual, but he was taking me off task and trying to scare me. I said no, and I paid attention to how he just rolled right over my answer, with zero respect. *Zero.* That was all I needed to see. This same coworker tried to dump a troubled case in my lap with the wrong protocol instruction, and again I stood up to him and said no. Without your Self Offense message in my head, at three in the morning (when, rightfully, everyone is tired), I would not have had the clarity to see the character of the person I was working with. I have since left that job and moved on to an incredible opportunity. I was able to calmly and rationally see respect in real time. Respecting someone's boundaries is everything in all relationships.

Zelda's Story

Home for the summer between her sophomore and junior year, my daughter Zelda bounced into the apartment on a steamy Friday afternoon. She had been shopping and was excited to share her purchases with me, along with the exciting news that she had a date with a young man she had just met.

"We're going out tonight—and he's definitely a 10."

I thought to myself, *Oh, God, please save us from the dreaded 10s of the world.* I took a deep breath and reminded myself that she has taken the Self Offense workshops, and that I trusted her. I said, as lightly as I could muster, "Great! Make sure you find something to say no to." When she got home that night, I asked her how the date went.

"Not that great."

"What happened?"

"We met up and walked around, and then we stopped in a park and sat on a bench. As we were talking, he put his hand on my thigh, and I thought, *Okay, here is my first 'no' opportunity.* In a very polite way—not at all bitchy—I gently moved his hand from my thigh.

"Mom, how he was being in that moment—his response—was kind of put off, like it was a problem that I did that. And how he reacted to my nonverbal but very clear 'no' was all I needed to know that I was not going to let myself be alone with him. I wasn't afraid of him, I didn't think he was going to attack me, but I was a little on my guard. From there, we went to the restaurant. At the end of the meal, I excused myself to use the restroom. It was one of those unisex restrooms, and—don't you know—he followed me into the restroom. We were the only two there, and he pushed me up against the wall to kiss me, and this time I said 'no' aloud and pushed him back.

"He again got kind of shitty with me, like I owed him something. He said we could go back to his place. I said, 'No thanks,' and gave him an excuse about how I had to get up early to work. That was pretty much how it ended. Mom, I don't think he was going to attack me; I don't even think he was a bad guy. I just didn't like how he reacted when I set the boundary—when I said no.

"He just wasn't listening, and I wasn't going to let myself be vulnerable with him. And I certainly wasn't going to go to his place, where he would have the home-field advantage."

Saving Face

Self-defense expert Shihan Gene Dunn and I co-taught a Self Offense and self-defense workshop a few years back in which he introduced the idea of "saving face," or avoiding humiliation. Originally, it was in the context of self-defense as a de-escalation tactic in the face of potential attack, but we discovered that it could also be a great offensive strategy—saying no to someone in a way that is gracious and gives that person an easy way to save face, especially in public. This is easy when things are going smoothly, but it can be challenging when someone says something that is upsetting, rude, offensive, or vulgar, and you want to lash out or put them in their place. This urge is valid and, for many of us, an automatic reaction.

In Self Offense, we're asking you to consider not taking that bait. Don't retaliate. Don't fight fire with fire. You could call it an act of pure generosity and graciousness. This kind of no—one that saves face—is a kind and compassionate way to allow the other person to exit the interaction with their dignity intact. This is you choosing to elevate rather than diminish another human being (and yourself)—even when you might not think that they deserve it, that you should have to, or that it will do any good. This is particularly important in public, where the stakes and the risk of conflict escalation are higher.

Remember back to when you were in high school and you asked someone to dance and they said no—or, worse, laughed? Or you were picked last for the softball or basketball team? Or the first time you raised your hand in school to answer a question and you got it wrong? Or you offered an idea at a work meeting and it got dismissed out of hand? How much worse was that experience because other people witnessed your failure? Or because you were ridiculed for having the temerity to ask or put yourself forward? You might have wanted to retaliate to make the other person feel bad—or at least to divert the attention away from your own embarrassment.

This same dynamic can play out in workplace harassment or in catcalling situations in the street. When someone addresses you in a way that does not work for you—maybe it is diminishing, offensive, or teasing, or it makes you feel unsafe—and they do so publicly, it raises the emotional stakes of the interaction. When we return another person's unwanted attention with shaming or anger, it can escalate the situation, up the ante. They feel they have no choice but to defend themselves or attempt to put you in your place.

If you respond to a derisive comment with something inflammatory, you could be setting yourself up for a fight. Of course, if fighting is how you want to deal with it, that is your prerogative, and you should be prepared to own it and the consequences that come with that choice. But responding kindly, leaving the other human being better or bigger than you found them, is also a choice. It is an act of generosity, and you will also be left better for yourself and bigger—and it may save you needless trouble.

This is not the same thing as condoning inappropriate behavior or being a doormat. Allowing someone to save face only works if you own it as an action you are taking, not something that you have been victimized by or are obligated to do. We find that a good question to ask yourself is *Would I rather be safe or right?* Either way, own it. We stand by you.

Michelle's Story

On the subway one afternoon, I sat beside a man who began leering at me out of the corner of his eye. "Mama, you are hot. I have somebody waiting at home, but, for you, I'll let her know that I'll be late." Now, it was a full subway car in the middle of the afternoon; I wasn't in any danger. But it was inappropriate, and I was being singled out in front of people. I could have shamed him. I could have said, "Screw you!" or "Are you kidding me?" or "How dare you?" Or I could have ignored him in an obvious way and sought out the agreement of the nearby passengers. Any or all of those reactions would have been valid—but also a potential provocation or challenge. Instead, I said, "Thank you. That is very flattering, but I'm gonna pass on that." I said it firmly and kindly. He said, "Okay," and went back to his business.

It cost me nothing to do this. I was proud of myself for handling it this way. Not because it was the right thing to do but because it was consistent with who I hold myself out to be. And it worked.

Olivia's Story

As a dental receptionist, I receive phone calls every day from companies or people trying to sell us goods and services. When I first started the job, I hated saying a flat no to the companies because there was either an attitude coming from the other line or because it would launch them into a "Please don't say no" speech. Now I always say, "We're not interested, but thank you for calling, and we hope you have a great day." I rarely receive any friction or speeches from them. They usually respond with, "Oh, thank you, have a nice day." It is so empowering to know a way to convey rejection and say no while still keeping a light energy in the conversation—especially because a no can easily lead to retaliation.

REFLECTION AND PRACTICE

- Can you think of a time when you went out of your way to say no to someone in a way that left them honored and appreciated?

- Notice all the ways that you say no in life, verbally and non-verbally, without actually saying the word *no*.

- When you do say the word *no*, notice what else is present that allows for that. Are you angry or upset in some way? Is it awkward or easy? What makes it that way? Is there a power imbalance? Notice the circumstances and the context in which no is communicated.

- Once a day, or the next time you speak to someone that you don't know well, find something to say no to. You can always change your mind afterward.

- Practice finding ways to say no that communicate a clear refusal and leave the other person honored and appreciated.

3

Welcome to
the Interview

We understand that we're not always confident saying no, and for good reason. We also understand that when we're not comfortable saying no, we can say or do other things to communicate no, and that even though those communications may be indirect, they are communicating no. Great. You may be asking yourself, "So what do I do with that?"

In chapter 1, I referred to context as an essential tool, and now I am going to give you a context to assess situations. It's called the Interview, and you're going to learn how to use it to assess the level of safety or trustworthiness of any interaction. An interview is defined as:

- A formal consultation, usually to evaluate qualifications (as of a prospective student or employee)
- A meeting at which information is obtained (as by a reporter, television commentator, or pollster) from a person

One of my favorite cartoon characters is Bugs Bunny. I am both amused by and envious of his ability to produce a literal rabbit hole out of his "pocket" (it's not like he's wearing pants). Whenever he needs to disappear out of a sticky situation, he throws a rabbit hole on the floor, ground, or air in front of him and then disappears into it. We can use context as a tool metaphorically in much the same way.

In Self Offense, the "rabbit hole," or context, that we can pull out to test people or situations is that of an Interview. In Gavin de Becker's book *The Gift of Fear,* the context of Interview is introduced to provide insight into the dynamic between people who mean harm and those they target. We are asked to consider that there is a selection process, and in the law enforcement industry it is referred to as an interview. Therefore, when you are selected as a possible target, a kind of interview is underway—you are being interviewed for your potential as a target or a person easy to harm: a victim. The assailant needs to know that they can control or dominate you, and your ability to be easily persuaded or manipulated or convinced to comply will be a key factor in their determination of whether you are a good target. If you are easily controlled now, it is likely you will be easily controlled later.

Recall the scenario from *The Gift of Fear* at the beginning of chapter 1, with the good Samaritan who was so eager to help with Kelly's groceries. Kelly was being interviewed for the "job" or "role" of victim, and everything the man in the stairwell said was to determine whether he could control her and get her to do what he wanted her to do—be alone with him by getting her into her apartment. Kelly passed his interview. She qualified for the job of victim, and he knew this because he was able to successfully manipulate her and talk her out of her no. We can assume that she passed other tests that were important to his objective. He likely knew that she lived alone and she was his "type."

You may be asking yourself, *So I just wait around until someone asks me for something or to do something, and then I remember to say no? I have to wait to be interviewed to practice this?* No—now that you have the Interview as a context, and you can see it from the point of view of the person who means harm interviewing their potential target, you can use this information to take the next step and be proactive by finding something to say no to. Effectively, *you are turning the Interview around so that you are now interviewing them.* I recommend that you find something to say no to as early as possible, to determine how the person you are interacting with will respond to your no. A good example of this kind of vetting is Olivia's girlfriend's story, as told to Olivia and shared with us.

> This is my girlfriend's story. She also took the course. She and her sister have not spoken to their father in about six years, but my girlfriend recently decided to contact him again without her mother or sister knowing. She took about two weeks to draft the first letter to him in which she included a whole paragraph just focused on her boundaries. She said that his respect for her boundaries is the most important part of restarting their relationship. If he starts breaking her boundaries or trying to talk her out of her boundaries in any way, she has made it clear that will be the end of their communication. I asked her why, and she said that it was because of this course. She knows that if he breaks her boundaries now, that means he hasn't grown and is in it for his own reasons and well-being, not hers. She also said that being in control of her boundaries makes her feel in control of the whole situation. If he breaks her boundaries, it's not worth staying.

There is no limit to who you can turn the Interview around on. You could go as far as turning the Interview around on anyone and everyone that you come into contact with in your life. Or you can save it for specific settings like dating, making new friends, or recruiting new business partners. Here is another example from Olivia:

> One of my friends from elementary school reached out to reconnect, and I was so excited to see him again. When we were at dinner, he asked if I wanted to go to his friend's house afterward, and I declined. He kept asking me, "Why not?" "What are you gonna do for the rest of the night?" "Are you really just gonna go home?" "So I'm gonna have to go by myself?" I was sort of interested in going, but after his reaction, I knew he wasn't someone I wanted to spend time with anymore. We hadn't seen each other in over ten years, and he was already treating my boundaries as optional. I went home that night, and thankfully he never reached out to me after that. My friends told me that a couple of weeks later he was kicked out of a party for breaking things and starting a fight, so I felt even more validated in my decision to create distance. The technique of telling someone no off the bat and just testing to see their reaction is an amazing way to quickly read someone's character.

Go ahead and turn that Interview around on as many or as few people as you like. Interview them for the privilege of being in your life, even if just for a moment. Proactively find something to say no to, and then observe their response to that boundary-setting, that no you have offered. This may be all you need to communicate that you are too much trouble in the face of a potential assailant or, as in Olivia's story, someone that you are very likely better off without. An assailant with limited time and access may abandon all effort if it looks like it will take too long to convince you, or the opportunity to do that unobserved has passed. You could say that communicating no is a way to fight with words, and that your willingness to fight with words can be seen as a deterrent for anyone looking to prey on you, like the lion who separates the weak and old from the herd of healthy mature antelope. It also has the power to reveal a more sinister intention by staging a verbal combat in the first location of contact, where you have a better chance of survival.

In the stairwell scenario, Kelly says no many different times and in many ways, but because she did not have the tool of using a pro-active no to turn the Interview around, she didn't take an action in the face of not being listened to. She got talked out of her no and she continued to go along with what the man in the stairwell told her to do. But if she had the tool of turning the Interview around and had seen that he was not going to listen to her, from there she could have taken a different action. She could have said her no with the specific intention to notice whether he honored her boundary, and when he didn't, she could have had that specific information to inspire her next action. Armed with evidence that this person was not likely to honor her boundary-setting, she could have refused to move farther up the stairs, or left her groceries on the stairs and headed back outside on the street, where there were likely other people. She might have thanked him for his offer to help, and told him that it is against her religion to allow an unknown man to assist her, and then offered to move aside so he could continue on his way to the fourth floor, where he said he was headed. She might have lied and said that her best friend was on the way while she sat down on the stairs and repacked her groceries, or if it had happened in this day and age, she might take out her phone and asked if he was okay with her taking a picture of him—since he was such a good Samaritan. It's not about what she would have done, it's about where she would have been thinking from. Similarly for you, it's not about memorizing responses or coming up with premade choices of what you do, but rather applying the tools to your own interactions and trusting that you will make the best decision for you in the moment based on whether they are listening to you or not. And you will have real-time evidence of that because you will have tested them in the moment instead of relying on a feeling or a sense of whether you should or shouldn't trust them.

If she had stuck to her no in the stairwell, he would have had to do one of two things: either he would have given up and left her alone, or he would have had to force her physically to do what he wanted or use physical force in the stairwell. We can assume that, because of the location of the interaction, the assailant must determine quickly whether Kelly will be a good choice for being his victim or target, and if she had persisted with her no, it's possible that he would have decided she wasn't a good choice. Why? Because he is also in a vulnerable position: he's in a public place, where at any moment someone visiting or who lives in the building could happen on them in the stairwell, and he could be discovered as someone who doesn't have any business being there. Therefore, he might have reckoned she'd be too much trouble, and it would not be worth the risk where he could be found out or witnessed. People in our workshops often point out that her persistence with her no could have provoked a violent response in him. My answer to that is that if a violent response was provoked, it would have happened in the stairwell, where the odds were in Kelly's favor, instead of in the apartment.

If someone is pushing back or resisting your no, I want you to notice that and factor it into your overall and moment-to-moment assessment of this person. The tricky thing about this is that people push back and resist our no's often—even when they don't mean us any harm. It's why Kelly likely didn't even notice that she wasn't being listened to—she likely just experienced being persuaded or pressured by a charming young man, and ultimately acquiesced to his requests to help her, and let him into her apartment. However, once you activate turning the Interview around by proactively finding something to say no to, when you see that they are not getting your no, you can end the interaction, or take a new action that empowers you in the face of what is happening—including doing nothing more than taking note of it. Even choosing to do nothing will empower you, because it will be you who is actively making that choice, and you will have a better idea of what to do next, rather than remaining uncertain.

In the practice of Self Offense, we proactively apply the context of an interview to the interactions that take place between people. We strongly recommend that you use it on first meeting someone, and then again, and as often as you need, when entering new levels or phases of intimacy or risk in your relationships—for example, moving from a platonic to a sexual relationship, or going into business with someone, or when hiring a caregiver or choosing a medical professional.

You can pull this tool from your pocket, just as Bugs Bunny does his rabbit hole, and use it whenever you want to test someone in a relationship for their willingness to listen to, respect, and honor your boundaries. If someone doesn't intend you harm, your saying no will still serve to set a boundary and give you insight as to how this person will respond to you disagreeing or setting limits with them. Once you trust that someone is open and respectful of your limit-setting, you are still free to change your mind or to say yes. I will say more about this in the next chapter.

Laura's Story

I'm at Webster Hall, in New York City, dancing in the basement club like a maniac when a superhot guy with muscly arms holds eye contact with me and makes his way over. We're both pretty drunk and soon we are very close, making out and writhing around in the middle of the crowd. About an hour later he asks me to go home with him and it turns out we both live in Hell's Kitchen, about a block apart! We dash out of the club, and as we make our way to the subway, he makes fun of a lady's coat, walking the other direction. I get a bad feeling in my gut and remember, *I don't know this guy at all.* Fear starts to flood my system, and then I remember the no test from Self Offense.

"David, I don't think I want to go home with you tonight. We just met and I wanna slow down a bit." I wait for his response, for him to tell me just what kind of person he is when he experiences rejection. He nods in disappointment and says he understands and asks for my number so we can go out another time. I put my number in his phone and he waves shyly and dashes off. I suddenly realize—he did great! He did exactly what I would want a guy to do, respect my no. I turn to look at him and from ten feet away he turns back and we lock eyes. "Hey, wait," I yell out to him. "Come back. I changed my mind!" We kiss and head to his place for a delicious conclusion.

The story above is an example of finding something to say no to, even when all you want to do is say yes, so that you can be confident in your choice to either stick with your no or change your mind.

Michelle's Story

It's Friday evening at 8:30 p.m. and I'm waiting for the subway to head home. I'm standing on the sparsely populated platform at West 4th Street in New York City waiting for the A train. The train pulls up, and as the door opens and I step on the train, I can feel a presence. My Spidey sense is activated and I turn around and lock eyes with a very handsome man. I am startled by the degree of intimacy and chemistry that is present. It is the proverbial "their eyes met from across the room" kind of experience.

I quickly look away and find a seat and begin to put in my headphones. He sits down across from me, and I can sense him looking at me. Out of the corner of my eye, I can see that he is smiling. I am afraid to look him directly in the eyes; I feel vulnerable, and it seems so intimate. Instead, I look at his shoes. Then I look at his knee. Then I look at his wrist. The whole time I am saying to myself, *For goodness' sake, look up! Look him in the eyes; you can do it!* I brace myself to look him in the face, and when I do he is right there smiling at me, and we both laugh. Pure magic.

I blush and look away again. We ride along in this bubble of chemistry until we get to my stop. I stand up, look down at him and I say, "Thank you, that was so much fun." He smiles again and then to my delight and simultaneous horror he stands up—and we leave the train together.

Now that little voice in my head is screaming at me, *Are you insane? You idiot! He could be a killer. You lead Self Offense; you know what you have to do. You have to find something to say no to.* But the thing was, I didn't want to say no to anything. What if that puts him off? What if he gets offended? What if I hurt his feelings? What if I make this amazing feeling go away or wreck my chances on romance before it has the space to be fulfilled?

As we're walking, we exchange names. We both marvel at the instant connection we feel and the uniqueness of our shared experience. We exit the subway station, walking together, and as we get to my street corner, I stop and prepare to say good-bye. He says, "You should give me your phone number." And I suddenly see my opportunity to say no. I say, "Tell you what, why don't you give me your number and I will contact you?" and then I wait and watch for his response. He smiles again. "Sure." He gives me his number and walks away. I am thrilled that he accepted my no to giving him my number and accepted my counteroffer and gave me his.

A counteroffer is a great no wrapped in a yes. So is disagreeing with someone by offering a contradicting or alternate point of view or opinion. I was proud of myself: proud that I took an action that was out of my comfort zone (saying no when I wanted to say yes) and standing for my own safety over feeling good in the moment. I left that initial interaction with some confidence in pursuing our getting to know each other further. I texted him the next day.

These are great examples of effectively turning the Interview around. But you might be asking yourself, *What if I let myself be talked out of my no? Like I forget to keep saying no, or it seems like no big deal to change my mind.* First of all, if you did get talked out of your no, it's great that you noticed it—that means you can be on the lookout for something to say no to going forward. Keep in mind that, in every interaction, we are training the people in our life in what they can expect of us, and you may have just trained that person to know that you can be talked out of your no. Not a problem, but you will likely need to work harder— and by working harder, I mean you will either need to be more direct or persistent—to have your no be accepted the next time. And knowing that you may have to work a little harder to get your no accepted will make a difference when that time comes. The following story is an example of my being talked out of a no and then having to work harder to have it accepted.

> I was headed to my dojo on 18th Street in New York City. It was a beautiful day with lots of people out on the streets heading to work, to lunch, or on various daily errands. I had been at a great sample sale and was carrying two big shopping bags, one in each hand. While I wasn't struggling, I certainly looked like I could use a hand.
>
> A very handsome young man came up beside me and offered to help me carry my bags, and even as I was saying, "No

thank you, I'm good," he was taking the bags from my hands. I went along with it and let him override or talk me out of my no as I let go of the bags. We walked side by side, talking about the beautiful day, and I am thinking to myself, *OMG. I teach Self Offense, and this is how I am handling this situation?*

We reached the street entrance to my third-floor dojo and he said, "I can bring them upstairs for you." Aha! Here it is, another opportunity to say no. So, I said, "No, thank you so much, but no, no, thank you." He said, "Are you sure? I don't mind." I said, "Yes, I am sure, thank you." He looked a bit confused and persisted: "Really, I don't mind."

I said, "I really got that. I can take it from here, thanks." We stood there for a moment. I looked directly at him, kindly, firmly, and most importantly, confidently in my persistence. He said, "Okay. Have a great day." I said, "Thanks, you too," and I watched him walk down the street.

I was prepared to have to work a little harder to have my no understood as I had given it up earlier—effectively training him that my no wasn't necessarily a firm boundary, even if he heard me say it. He seemed like a genuinely helpful person, and this was a good opportunity for me to practice saying no and hold firmly and kindly in a low-stakes situation.

The following is another story from Olivia asserting her no in an already established friendship after she took our Self Offense workshop.

My college roommate and I lived together for two years. We were close friends at first, but about two months into living together, I just felt like my opinion wasn't as valued as hers in the friendship. Things were often done "her way or the highway," and as someone who usually goes with the flow, it didn't bother me at all at first. I think this created a dynamic where she wasn't often told no, and when I did say no, she would get quite frustrated with me and try to talk me out of it. It got to a point where I stopped saying no—or she took away my no—because it was easier to do what she wanted than to deal with her anger. Living with someone like this over time made me feel really small. Toward the end of the second year of living together, I started creating distance and saying no more often despite the consequences. Eventually, she asked to end the friendship because she felt like I had lost interest in the friendship and started fighting against her. I actually just started treating her like I treated all of my other friendships, where I said no as often as I needed to and hung out with other friends with no thought of any consequences.

You may find that when you get authentic in your relationships and start saying no and setting boundaries where you have been scared or reluctant to do so, some relationships may end suddenly or slowly fade away. While this can be uncomfortable and even sad, hang in there, as new spaces open up for relationships with people who are aligned with you and respectful of your boundaries. You get to say who does and doesn't deserve to be in your life.

REFLECTION AND PRACTICE

Practice actively using the context of an Interview when meeting new people, or in new situations with friends, family, coworkers, acquaintances, and strangers. Turn the Interview around by proactively finding something to say no to and see what they do.

Practice noticing in your interactions whether someone is listening to you. Ask yourself:

- Is this person listening to me?
- Are they accepting or pushing back on my boundaries?

- Is this person preventing me from taking actions that support my well-being?

- Do I feel safe, or do I feel uneasy, like I am walking on eggshells?

Quid Pro Quo

noun. 1. A favor or advantage granted or expected in return for something.

The decision to say no or not is often influenced by the dynamics of "what is owed" and subtle or implied transactions. When you do a favor for someone, do you expect them to do a favor for you in return? When someone does you a favor, do you feel that you owe them a favor in return? Many of us would say no to the first question and yes to the second question. Me too, until one day I had the following insight while going about my day in Manhattan.

I like to hold open doors for people at the deli, at the gym, at the movie theater—pretty much anywhere. Now let's be clear, no one appointed me Official Door Opener and Holder for all of Manhattan, and obviously I don't get paid. I hold the door open for others because it is consistent with my view of myself as a good person who enjoys being of service to others. I don't expect anything in return—or so I thought. Then one day, I notice that whenever someone passes through the door that I am so generously holding open for them, and they do not say "thank you," I sarcastically say to myself, *You're welcome!* Which is followed quickly by the thought, *Really? You are just going to walk through the door and not say anything? Who do you think you are?*

Ha! Apparently, I do expect something in return after all. I expect a thank-you or some kind acknowledgment, a smile or a nod, in return for my service. Once I saw that I had this expectation, and I owned it as an expectation rather than a rule that everyone should follow, I was free to hold a door open and accept that people are free to acknowledge it or not.

I am bringing this to your attention not to be cynical about people's intentions but rather to highlight the transactional nature inherent in many of our interactions. Consider that when you do someone a favor or accept a kindness, an unspoken expectation gets created, and you are now in a kind of social debt. And unless you have negotiated differently up front, you may find that there are unspoken expectations by you or others that you want to be wary of, and this may impact your experience of freedom to set a boundary or say no.

It is not that you shouldn't accept the generosity of another human being. If you have any concern for an implied quid pro quo when presented with gifts of dinner, drinks, assistance, and so on, you can say no or make a counteroffer.

Imagine going on a date and having the freedom to say up front, "Are you expecting me to buy dinner, or will we split the check?" Or, "I would like to buy you dinner in exchange for the pleasure of your company." Now, many people might think, *What? That's so weird,* but only because we are not used to directly dealing with the subtle transactional nature of our interactions. If you aren't empowered to say no or to have an honest conversation about expectations, then you might want to reconsider being involved with this person or situation, or you may have to prepare yourself for a more awkward or difficult boundary-setting later on.

Where we get into sticky situations is when the expectations are unspoken or assumed, and we feel pressured by them. Or we don't want to be seen as someone who operates transactionally because we have a moral judgment about that and we don't want to look bad to ourselves or others, even though most of us operate this way at least some of the time. Situations where this might show up are when you are deciding who pays for dinner when you are on a date. Or at mealtime with your roommates or life partner, where it is unspoken but expected that whoever makes dinner doesn't have to do the dishes. Your kids don't get dessert unless they eat their vegetables, and you don't get dessert unless you spend thirty minutes on the treadmill. I was married with the understanding that my husband would provide financial support, and it was up to me to be the social director and manage child care and household chores. I think if we tell the truth, we all operate like this at some level. Our relationships and our lives are filled with subtle transactions like these. Some are more accepted and agreed on among large groups—what is considered to be good manners, or the social contract—and some are specific to certain situations or individuals and their associated values. I'm not saying that is a problem, or that there are some transactions that are better or safer than others. I'm asking that we *notice when a transaction is present* so that it does not become the unspoken or implied leverage for you to do something that you would not otherwise do and that ultimately causes you harm.

If we think back to the situation with Kelly in chapter 1, there is a subtle transaction that is adding social pressure to the situation. Because he helps her with her groceries, she is assumed to be in his debt, and therefore she may feel obligated to continue to interact with him and even allow him into her apartment—otherwise she is seen as ungrateful for his assistance.

As a general rule, if you do need assistance—for example, those times when you need help getting your carry-on in or out of the overhead compartment, or when you are in a foreign location and you need directions—it is safer for you to do the asking. Asking a random person to assist you carries less risk than accepting assistance offered by someone you don't know. And when someone does stop you to ask for directions or offers to assist you unsolicited, you can always say no to test their intentions. They may respond with "Are you sure?" but beyond that, they should listen. And remember, once they pass this listening test, you can always change your mind.

REFLECTION AND PRACTICE

- In those places where you spend the most time, such as the offce, school, or home, practice noticing your own expectations for compensation or acknowledgment in exchange for your actions.

- The next time someone fails to say "thank you" when you think you deserve it, practice noticing your own reactions, big or small.

- When someone offers to do you a favor, buy you a drink or dinner, or give you a gift, consider what might be their expectation for that kindness. If you suspect that it is more than a thank-you or anything beyond what you are willing to reciprocate, either refuse the kindness or consider addressing the expectation up front.

- What is this idea of quid pro quo provoking for you?

4

Teddy Bear or Teddy Bundy? Unpacking Unconscious Bias

One of the early lessons in martial arts is that you can't judge a person by the color of their belt.

You would think that the most dangerous people in the dojo are the black belts. They have the most skill, the most experience, and are potentially the most lethal. In fact, the most dangerous people in the dojo are the white belts, the beginners. They are both unpredictable and unskilled in their practice and therefore at the highest risk for hurting themselves and others as they learn how to blend speed and power with judging distance, intention, and form. They also have the least experience practicing martial arts under duress and are therefore most likely to react unpredictably in fear and surprise. The black belt is skillful and can execute techniques in a way that both challenges and protects their partner. The white belt is far more dangerous than the black belt—the polar opposite of what most of our unexamined perceptions of martial artists would tell us.

I have a dear friend, Shihan Maria, who is a highly accomplished and respected colleague in the martial arts. We trained and co-taught together for many years. She is a high-ranking teacher in both full-contact Japanese karate and Eizan Riu Jiujitsu, where she has been the chief instructor for decades. Early in the creation of our Self Offense workshops, she taught the Self-Defense portion. She is also a mom with a great sense of humor. She is in her early sixties, about 5-foot-3, and wears glasses and sensible boots.

She has the gnarly fingers that come from years of teaching and practicing gripping, grappling, punching, and throwing people bigger than her. If you saw her on the streets of the Lower East Side, where she has lived for decades, based on how she looks, you would likely think that she was a defenseless and slightly cranky-looking Goth librarian. You would be surprised to learn that she often carries a knife hidden in her boot, that she knows how to use it, and that she can easily flip a man twice her size.

Looks are deceiving. If you think you will know the person who intends to harm you by how they look, you are mistaken. In fact, you are most vulnerable to those who *don't* fit your casting office description of an "evil, smarmy person" because you likely already have your guard up around the people that you think "look dangerous." A famous example of this was the serial killer Ted Bundy, who used his charm, good looks, and a fake broken arm to entrap and then murder women. He preyed on their sympathy and kindness and counted on them not being threatened by an injured, defenseless, handsome man. He approached them with his arm in a sling and requested assistance.

When we are attracted to someone or flattered by their attention, it can be the most difficult time to keep our guard up or to say no, especially as a test. When we really want to say yes, the emotional stakes are high. To say no, we have to resist what feels natural and desirable in that moment in favor of the more calculated no response.

If you find yourself in this position, wanting to say yes, it can help to remind yourself that saying no up front to test someone's intentions, to see what they do with your no, can save you trouble down the road. And it could even save your life.

For this, write down in your journal the first thing that comes to mind. Don't overthink it.

Part 1

Imagine the person of your dreams, your ideal mate.

1. What gender are they?
2. How old are they?
3. What socioeconomic class are they?
4. Are they your good friend?
5. What is their religion?
6. What color skin do they have?
7. How do they dress?
8. What is their main personality trait? Funny? Charming? Smart?

Part 2

Now imagine the person who stalks you, assaults you, attacks you, perpetrates harm against you.

1. What gender are they?
2. How old are they?
3. What socioeconomic class are they?

4. Are they your good friend?

5. What is their religion?

6. What color skin do they have?

7. How do they dress?

8. What is their main personality trait?

Part 3

Now ask yourself:

1. Which of those two people is the more desirable to me?

2. Which of those two people am I more vulnerable to?

Most people who do this exercise find that the person they imagine as their ideal mate is more attractive or appealing than the person they imagine preying upon them. The exercise can also uncover our automatic unconscious biases. For example, we may believe the person who causes harm is male (perhaps because we assume men are more capable of violence than women—not an unreasonable assumption, statistically, but an assumption nonetheless) or someone who is older than us (perhaps because we associate youth with innocence) or a different race or culture than we are (perhaps because we've grown up to believe that people who look like us, have the same color skin, worship at the same altar, or have the same level of education are safer than those who do not).

There are a couple of takeaways here. Generally, we think that there are physical markers or recognizable characteristics that we can use to identify good people from bad people. Often that is based on how danger has looked in the past, what we have been taught by our culture or parents, what we have heard from others, or what we have seen in movies and on TV. In truth, what we think a "bad" person looks like is inaccurate. You are more vulnerable to the person who resembles your ideal person because you are less likely to have your guard up in the first place.

We think that we will recognize a safe person when we see them, but these can also be the people with whom it is hardest to set boundaries. When you are with that more desirable person, or someone you want to think well of you, you probably really want to say yes, especially when it seems like you both really like each other. Who wants to risk messing with the start of a beautiful friendship, a hot hookup, or a promising business opportunity or collaboration by saying no?

Ultimately, people should be judged by their actions, not by their appearance, which is why you want to give them an opportunity to show you their actions by finding something to say no to and seeing what they do. Someone can appear nice, or well-dressed, or kind-spoken, and still not have our best interest at heart. Nice, well-dressed, well-educated, and fully employed does not equal a good person any more than poorly dressed, uneducated, unemployed, and rude equals a bad person. Being able to identify your biases and associations with "good" and "bad" people will help you to identify when someone truly is or isn't trustworthy or potentially dangerous.

This is why I recommend you go beyond your first impressions and instead use no as a test. You may have already had the experience of being with someone who seemed really great until you said no to them, and then they stopped being great. They got angry or dismissive or disapproving. It's likely those past experiences are what have you hesitate to say no or set boundaries in the present. I also recommend that where you practice setting boundaries is with people that you are attracted to, want to get to know, and want in your life, and that you practice it early on in getting

to know them. You likely already have plenty of practice saying no
with those you think look dangerous or undesirable, but less with
those you think are amazing from the start.

REFLECTION AND PRACTICE

- What hidden or obvious bias are you noticing? Note cultural,
  gender, and socioeconomic preferences or aversions.

- What are some stereotypes that you hold as true? For example, all people of color are dangerous, all white people are
  entitled, gay men are weak, old white men in power are
  untrustworthy, women are overly emotional.

- What are some instances when you've been wrong about
  your implicit biases?

The more authentic and specific you can be in answering
these questions for yourself, the more useful this exercise will be in
empowering you to stay safe and aware in your interactions. This
is not a place for you to judge or blame yourself for your biases or
preconceived notions. Give yourself the freedom to discover them
and examine them as they are—ideas, thoughts, memories, inherited
conclusions, and past experiences—and maintain compassion
for yourself.

Working with Intuition

Living in New York City has given my Spidey sense lots of practice. I have crossed the street to avoid wacky talkers and yellers,
made excuses not to step into an elevator when I got a negative

vibe from a person mumbling to themselves, or ducked into a store and let the clerk know that I was being followed and I needed to browse until the coast was clear. I have stood up, changed seats, and then changed cars on the subway when a man sat down across from me and glared at me. I don't know if any one of these people would have caused me physical harm. I do know that the actions I took were my way of saying no to the situation, and that taking action is empowering.

As a young teenager walking the three miles home from my baseball game, I refused an offer of a ride from a stranger because it gave me a bad feeling. To this day, whenever I recall watching him drive off and turn the opposite direction of where he said he was going, I think that gut feeling saved my life.

A lot has been written about this mechanism called intuition (or your gut, or sixth sense) and its role in keeping us safe or guiding us to make the right decisions. I'm pretty sure that you have been told at some point to trust yourself. However, have you ever had a feeling that something bad was going to happen, and then nothing bad happened? Or have you ever been blindsided by something bad happening with zero warning?

Our intuition, while valid and useful, is often insufficient. Our mind argues with our gut. You have likely had the experience where your Spidey sense got triggered in a social situation and you had thoughts like *Don't be so judgmental,* or *They'll think I'm rude,* or *They'll accuse me of being prejudiced,* or *I don't want to hurt their feelings,* or *I am being paranoid,* and then you acted contrary to what your intuition was telling you. Your thoughts overrode your intuition.

While I do want you to listen to your intuition, I also want you to have an action to take that is related to what is happening in the present moment of the situation that you find yourself in. An action that will help you verify what your intuition is telling you in a real way. As I've emphasized in earlier chapters, one way to do this is to find something to say no to. Confirm your intuition, one way or the other, with this action. This could be a verbal no to someone you are interacting with, or it could be a nonverbal no to the situation—like changing seats or moving away from someone and then seeing what happens.

If we look back at the situation from chapter 1 with Kelly in the stairwell, she likely had a moment of intuition when she noticed that her downstairs door had been left ajar. Though we don't know, we can speculate that Kelly thought it was strange—and she ignored her intuition that something was off and entered her building anyway. Who hasn't done something like that and had it all turn out fine? Let's look to see what we might do to say no to that situation of the door being left ajar. Maybe we can call a friend or neighbor and wait to be escorted into the building, or maybe we put the groceries down and enter the building with caution. Or we alert the building superintendent or even call the police. All these options are potentially inconvenient, or maybe embarrassing to have to do, especially when we don't know for sure that there is danger lurking, but they are actions to take to communicate no to the situation.

The point of this thought exercise is not to theorize on how Kelly *should* have handled the open door, but rather to point out that we override our intuition all the time—and that saying no to the situation may not be a convenient action to take. Again, I am not here to tell you what to do; I am here to give you a place to think from. You get to choose how you respond to your intuition, and I recommend you use it as a signal to find something to say no to so you can test it out in reality. Asking yourself, "How can I say no to this situation?" is a great place to start.

REFLECTION AND PRACTICE

If you experience an intuition that something is not quite right, stop and ask yourself the following:

- Where am I?

- What exits are available?

- Are there people close enough to hear me if I yell?

- Am I afraid to do something I normally would not be afraid to do?

- Am I carrying anything in my hand, like a phone or a water bottle or keys, that I can use as a weapon?

- If I am interacting with a person, are they listening to me and honoring my requests?

What is opening up for you in this chapter? What are you seeing for yourself regarding intuition and trusting your gut?

5

Manipulation: You Can't Make Me, or Can You?

Negging: Low-grade insults meant to undermine the self-confidence of a woman so that she might be more vulnerable to advances.*

Guilting: To persuade or induce someone to do something by causing feelings of guilt.†

Gaslighting: A psychological manipulation of a person, usually over an extended period, that causes them to question the validity of their own thoughts, perception of reality, or memories.**

---

*Urban Dictionary, s.v. "Negging," December 14, 2020, www.urbandictionary.com/define.php?term=Negging.

† Merriam-Webster Collegiate Dictionary, s.v. "guilt *(v.)*," accessed July 7, 2023, www.merriam-webster.com/dictionary/guilting.

** Merriam-Webster Collegiate Dictionary, s.v. "gaslighting *(n.)*," accessed July 7, 2023, www.merriam-webster.com/dictionary/gaslighting.

Time to stop pretending that we are all perfectly good people and start dealing with the degree to which we manipulate to get what we want. I don't mean to be accusatory, but if the shoe fits, go ahead and wear it; it's a popular shoe. We are especially likely to use these tactics in the face of someone saying no to us. In the face of no, most people will push back in response, with anything from a polite "Are you sure?" all the way up to a full-on confrontation. And this is what we can expect, even from the people we care about!

When I ask my daughter, Zelda, a technical question about posting on my Instagram that can be solved by Googling (and what question cannot be solved by Googling?), she calls me a "boomer" so that I will stop asking and leave her alone, and because I don't want to be seen as a useless dinosaur, I slink away and Google it. Zelda is triggering a response from me—I am reacting to not wanting to be seen as useless and old, by her or by me. She is not trying to harm me, and she is likely not even thinking to herself, *I am going to manipulate my mom into getting what I want*—it is just a part of the communication tactics that we inherited and use to get what we want from others or get people to do things they don't want to do.

What do people say to you when they want to get you to do something? It might be something that you are afraid is true about you that you want to prove wrong. Some examples could be, "Don't be so selfish," "cold," "uptight," "serious," or "paranoid." Or maybe you are known to "come to the rescue," and can always be counted on to say yes, and you don't want to disappoint.

These are Triggers and we all have them. They work to trigger a reaction in us. If you can't immediately see what your trigger is, ask a sibling, your partner, or a close friend to tell you the thing that they say to you to get you to do what they want or to make you feel a little guilty. You could also ask them which of your qualities or traits you are most defensive about. You may know theirs too, and if you do, it's probably because you use it to get what you want from them. I encourage you to bring a little lighthearted compassion to this inquiry.

This way of communicating is inherited. It was here before you and I were born and it will remain long after we are gone. It is deeply embedded in our ordinary and everyday interactions. It's automatic, passed down generation to generation, reinforced with families, siblings, and friends, and later in life it shows up between fellow students, coworkers, acquaintances, and in our intimate relationships. It survives because, like any tactic that serves to aid us in reaching our goals, it's useful. Manipulating helps us get what we want—it's how the media convinces us that we need the latest iPhone—so we don't get left behind or aren't seen as uncool. Sometimes it's subtle, like when your friend says, "We always do what you want to do," or more overt, like when your boss says, "You need to close this deal. We had to fire the salesperson who didn't make their quota."

You will also likely have more than one trigger, and it could be situational. For example, you may be someone who hates or is very uncomfortable around someone else crying. You feel that you have to do something about it; you want to fix it. So you will do whatever you can to make them, and you, feel better, or at least stop the crying. Another trigger could be when your heartstrings are being pulled—someone is invoking the loss of a loved one or other painful experience that you can relate to, and you are compelled to ease that pain, again, for both of you.

When we're triggered by manipulation, we feel compelled to act—either to deny what we're being accused of, or to fix the situation that is making us feel activated. If we refer to the story from chapter 1, the attacker says to Kelly, "There is such a thing as being too proud, you know." He is putting her down ever so slightly, accusing her of being too proud or stuck up to accept his help. He succeeds in this manipulation because Kelly doesn't want to be seen that way—she is successfully triggered and compelled to take an action that has her not appear "too proud," and she gives up her resistance, her no, and lets him help her. This communicates to him that with a subtle manipulation, he can control her, at least in this moment, and very likely in the future. He does it again when he says, "We can leave the door open like ladies do in old movies." He is implying that she is old-fashioned or overly cautious.

When people are manipulating you, it doesn't necessarily mean they want to harm you. They may just want what they want badly enough, and this is the way they know how to get it. They might not even realize that what they are doing is trying to manipulate you. What I want to leave you with is the ability to notice when you are feeling manipulated, so that you can do something about it in the moment and take an action that works for you and keeps you safe. It doesn't matter what your emotional trigger is; the point is to recognize it and own it. Be the author of it. Commit 100 percent to it. Whatever the response, it's your response. Whether you deflect, agree, counter-propose, question it, repeat it back to make sure you got it right, or walk away, commit to it. Whether you are a smart-ass, a goofball, or a sweetie-pie about it, own it. If, in our story, Kelly had said, "There's also such a thing as being too nosy, you jerk," or "I *am* proud. My mama taught me never to accept help from strangers, and I'm not starting today," or simply, "I don't think I'm too proud," and held her ground, he would have had to back down or escalate his assertion.

When you feel emotionally activated, another great practice is to listen for what might be driving another person's interaction with you: what their intention is, or why they are asking what they are asking. The trick is to authentically ask that question from what you think might be true for them. For example, when your friend wants you to go out and says some version of, "Don't be such a drag, let's go party," you might say, "It seems like you are really counting on me," or "You will be disappointed if I don't come with you," or "You want me to feel bad for not going out with you."

Using that approach, Kelly could have said, "Wow, helping a complete stranger with their groceries is really important to you," or "You really want me to accept your help. I'm not helpless, you know." These responses are ultimately Kelly saying no to him. She's not accepting the premise of the trigger, that she may be too proud. Her saying no in this way would have required him to give her more information in response—and who knows what else she would have discovered about his intentions, or whether he would have decided she was just too much trouble.

However you decide to practice this, I invite you to be compassionate and patient with yourself and others. Despite how it feels in the moment, mostly what we are saying no to is not a matter of life and death. And saying no when no is your truth brings respect, honor, and workability to your life, to you and the people with whom you engage. And remember, you are not saying no to them, you are saying no to what they are asking of you.

REFLECTION AND PRACTICE

Part 1

Begin by noticing what insecurities you have or aspects of your character people leverage to get you to comply with their wishes. What are you noticing about your emotional triggers and buttons?

Part 2

Write down what you think someone could say or has said to you that is triggering. Imagine what their intentions are behind the message. Then write possible responses. For example:

Your friend says, "Let's go out to a movie and then to a party," and you say, "No, I don't think so. I have a paper to write," and they reply in one of these ways:

- "You already get straight A's. What else do you have to prove?" They might be implying you are a show-off, or that your paper isn't that important.

- "You work too hard. You need to lighten up!" You imagine they mean you'll miss out on life if you spend too much time studying.

- "Come on, it won't be any fun without you!" They could mean you are not a good friend for not coming with them, or that they'd have a better time if you joined them.

You could respond like this:

- "Yes. Mmm. A's—I just love them. Can't get enough of those A's."

- "Yes. I am working hard now so that I can have a future of frivolous fun—which you will be invited to, if you leave me alone to do my work."

- "Thank you. I love being included. However, I am sticking to my plan to stay in and study."

All these responses communicate no and give you some ways to deal with the manipulation that aren't necessarily shutting the person down directly or escalating the interaction. You are also always welcome to say, "I said no." Do what works for you. Most of the time manipulations are harmless, and in case someone has sinister intentions, these communications allow you to stick with your no without necessarily escalating.

Part 3

Practice different responses in a mirror or with a trusted friend. If being a smart-ass is your style, you can try: "Me and my boring-ass-self are gonna write a brilliant paper, and then bask in the glory of a job well done," or "I feel for you and the bleak life you have laid out for yourself in my absence. Really. I do. Look at my sad face." Or you can forgo the smart-ass altogether and say kindly and directly, "I know. I got it. And I really cannot. Sorry." Mirror work, or practicing with a friend, can feel uncomfortable or weird, but remember, saying no is a muscle that we need to work often, and this can be a great way to do that. Give yourself permission to practice. It's worth it.

- Practice saying your response in the mirror with a straight face.
- Practice saying your response like you are in a soap opera.
- Practice singing your response like you are in an opera.
- Practice whispering your response like it's a big-deal secret.
- Practice saying your response like it's the saddest news ever.
- Practice saying your response like you just won the lottery.
- Have as much fun as humanly possible.

6

Physical Communication

How many of us have heard that all we need to do to be safe is to "be more aware"? We are advised to "look alert" and "pay attention to our surroundings." How do we actually *do* that? What actions can we take to be alert? What is the "doing" of being aware?

Let's begin with the definitions of *awareness* and being *alert.* According to Merriam-Webster's dictionary, *awareness* is defined as "knowledge and understanding that something is happening or exists." As I like to say it, noticing what is literally happening *as it is happening.* The word *alert* is defined as "a state of careful watching and readiness, especially for danger or opportunity." It is our awareness, our knowledge and understanding of what is happening around us, that *tells us to be alert.* They are two sides of the same coin.

For most of us, there is a baseline awareness that we maintain in public that serves to keep us from bumping into things or stepping out in front of traffic, and much of the time this baseline awareness is automatic; it exists in the background, like an autopilot. (Like when you drive all the way home without being able to recall the journey, or when you turn down a familiar street only to remember halfway there that your office is no longer on that street, or that you no longer work there.) This type of awareness is not what I am talking about when I refer to the "doing" of being alert. This level of awareness does not require you to actively "do" anything.

Self Offense focuses on two components of awareness and being alert that go beyond this baseline autopilot that will give you access to practicing the "doing" of being alert. The first component is the conscious actions you take to be alert when the situation calls for it.

This could look like scanning the environment, looking for exits, listening for footsteps, and so on. All of those actions are being done by you so that you experience yourself as "on alert" or actively paying attention. When you do these things, you will experience yourself as taking an action or "doing" something, even if it is only something that *you* know you're doing, or is only observable to you as the person doing it.

This brings us to the second component of practicing the "doing" of being alert, which is going beyond your personal experience of your own alertness and adding actions that communicate to others in your surrounding environment that you are alert. This could look like turning your head when looking around, instead of just using your peripheral vision, or taking out your earbuds when walking on the street late at night. These kinds of actions and gestures not only raise your ability to pay closer attention to your surroundings; they can also be seen from a distance and communicate to others in an obvious way that you are alert to your surroundings. When you take intentional and observable actions to be more alert and to communicate that you are more alert to others, you are practicing the "doing" of being alert.

You may be asking yourself, *Okay, so I'm communicating that I'm more alert, and I am acting more alert, but how is that going to keep someone from targeting me for an attack in the first place?* People do not observe you in a vacuum. When people observe you, they have assessments of you, your character, your capabilities, and your skill sets that they will make because you are taking or not taking these actions. Consider that by practicing the "doing" of being alert, you are projecting a level of intention and certainty that communicates that you potentially have a deeper training and knowledge about how to protect yourself, and are therefore not an easy target. If someone is going to attack you in the street or in an underground parking lot, they need you to be someone they can dominate quickly, someone who won't put up much of a fight. Think about it—they are in public, meaning anywhere outside your home, and the act of attempting to attack you carries with it a level of risk for them. Even if there aren't a lot of people around, there is still the possibility of being observed and caught in the act.

And here's the thing: By practicing the "doing" of being alert, you do have deeper training and knowledge of how to protect yourself than the average person walking around on autopilot. It's not a ruse for potential attackers. The average untrained person relies on being surprised to shift into being alert, and then has to react to active danger and figure out what actions to take to protect themselves under duress. You, on the other hand, are being proactive in this shift, and you therefore have a better shot at seeing trouble coming and at handling potential danger. This is the basis of Self Offense. Take proactive action, on a regular basis in your everyday life, to dramatically decrease the likelihood of being surprised by danger.

It is important to note that this type of paying attention, that I call the "doing" of being alert, is not the same as hypervigilance or living in fear. Hypervigilance is excessive alertness, as in going beyond what is necessary or rational for the situation. Additionally, being afraid and being alert are not the same thing, although it may feel the same because for many of us, being afraid is what prompts us to be alert. Now, you might be asking, *But, Michelle, couldn't this communication of my potential skills to protect myself actually make me stick out in a crowd more, and make me more likely to be picked?* It's possible, sure. But I'm going to offer that it is perhaps the right kind of sticking out because what sticks out is "Don't mess with me." What sticks out is your certainty of the situation and your confidence in your abilities, even when you may not feel confident in the moment. More on that later.

The Planes of Space and What They Communicate

As a Laban Certified Movement Analyst and professional martial artist, I have a lot that I could say on this topic. But to sum it up succinctly, I will say it in two ways: "Space rules," and "The person who dominates the space dominates the fight."

When it comes to space and how it communicates, we're not talking about a concept but rather a phenomenon that is palpable and highly contextual. It is not so much accessed through thinking, although you will have thoughts about space. Instead, it is experienced with your senses. When someone gets close to you, you sense it on a physical, even cellular level. It may be sensed before the words are there for you to describe it—then, depending on the context, you will determine whether the distance is appropriate, whether it is desirable or alarming. Space is to be experienced for oneself, not conceptualized or "understood." If you take on experiencing and sensing space, it will emerge as a potent player in your communications—one that can serve or undermine what you are out to communicate verbally and nonverbally. In the context of personal protection, you want to use your sensing of space to keep people at a distance, if appropriate, and you also want to be able to communicate your ownership of your personal space and your ability to set a boundary in the physical realm. This use of and understanding of space will help you set a boundary that has the power to communicate no from a safe distance. So, how do you communicate a boundary at a safe distance and still be able to interact with people? This is a sort of dance. It is dynamic and fluid, it shifts from partner to partner and situation to situation, and space is a major factor in that dance.

Our interactions take up physical space, and that shifts moment to moment in reaction and response to our inner and outer environments. This is distinct from how we use gestures, posture, or body language to communicate. There are many books and studies about nonverbal communication and how we use gestures, postures, and body language to communicate; a few can be found in the resources section at the end of this book. But I am not going to address that area of study here. I invite you to include it in your own analysis of how you occupy space and relate to others and your environment through the use of space, but I caution you against relying on your ability to read body language to keep yourself safe or to sense danger. Instead, throughout this section, I emphasize two spatial planes and the power they communicate all by themselves, without any influence from the person or element arranged in those planes: These planes are the plane of confrontation, toe-to-toe or face-to-face, and the plane of agreement, side-by-side.

Plane of Confrontation or Negotiation

If you recall from your fourth-grade geometry class, a plane is a two-dimensional shape. For example, what I refer to as the "plane of confrontation" or sometimes the "plane of negotiation" is called the sagittal plane. This is when two people are standing toe-to-toe and face-to-face. Imagine two gunslingers facing off in the *High Noon* position. Even if they start out back-to-back and slowly walk away from each other, they are setting up for a confrontation because they are on the same sagittal plane, even as they are walking away from each other. Once they hit their ten steps, they turn around and start shooting. They are very clearly on opposing sides, and not just physically; their objectives—to kill each other— are diametrically opposed.

This way of placing oneself in relationship to another is often unconscious and expresses the background context of the relationship that is playing out in the plane. On a less dramatic level, this is also observable between teacher-student, parent-child, and employee-boss—a.k.a. people who are in opposite roles. It shows up reliably among MMA fighters and boxers who amp up the rivalry by getting super close, face-to-face, and puffing out their chests at their pre-fight public weigh-ins. One of my favorite images of the stalemate potential of this arrangement is illustrated beautifully in the Dr. Seuss story "The Zax." Simply said, the North-going Zax and the South-going Zax meet face-to-face on a walk—each headed in the opposite direction and each one stubbornly refusing to step aside, out of the direct sagittal plane–type relationship, to let the other pass. An entire city grows up around them as they hold this toe-to-toe and face-to-face challenge. Fundamentally, being face-to-face and toe-to-toe in the sagittal plane is experienced as oppositional, and often, though not always, confrontational. On the flip side, this confrontational space can also be incredibly intimate, as the closer you get, the more "in someone's space" you are, and the more they are in yours. This fundamental coming-together of these opposing sides is what creates tension, which is sometimes very desirable. Like when you're watching the conclusion of a romance movie, and the two leads are slowly coming together, face-to-face, to finally kiss. You're screaming from your couch "Just kiss already!" because you can sense the intimacy and tension that is created in part through this spatial alignment.

For our purposes, the ongoing practice of noticing our spatial relationships as we communicate will give access to new actions that potentially de-escalate confrontation by literally changing the location of our communication as it relates to others. Changing where you are coming from physically will significantly change the dynamic of your interaction. Think of a time when you went to console a friend, and you placed yourself beside them. People trained as mental health workers are trained not to stand between their patients or clients and the door, particularly if the patient or client is agitated. Taking actions based on spatial alignment will give you some skills in de-escalating or exiting interactions that are nonverbally threatening or intimidating. The more you can start to see and understand spatial alignment, the more you will be able to use it to your advantage and notice when it is being used against you or in a way you are not okay with.

Side-by-Side:
The Plane of Agreement and Alignment

Contrast the sagittal confrontational plane with what we refer to as the "plane of alignment" or the "plane of we." For this plane, imagine you are standing side by side or you are seated next to someone. This spatial arrangement communicates that you are on the same side as the people you are standing or sitting next to. This alignment is observable in people waiting for the bus. They are all waiting for the bus, and all are observed as aligned, together in waiting. Another example is everyone at a sporting or theatrical event, seated side by side as the collective audience, all sharing an experience of the game or the show. My favorite image of the power of this alignment is when I see it at work in a group of teenagers—in my experience, often girls—walking down the hallway at school or on the street. They arrange themselves in a perfect side-by-side line, careful not to be even a little ahead or behind one another for fear of experiencing the subtle break in belonging that being out of this physical alignment can imply.

The Sweet Spot: 45 Degrees

Forty-five degrees is the sweet spot between the plane of confrontation and the plane of alignment. It conveys the dominance of the face-to-face plane of confrontation, but it is softened by being off to the side, as in the plane of alignment. You may recall seeing an image of a young school-age couple standing together. She is standing against the wall holding her books close to her chest. He is facing her but slightly off to her side. He has one arm up with his hand placed against the wall and above her head, creating a kind of fence around her. He is physically dominating the space around her, without being up in her face. She could experience this as protective and desirable, or she could experience it as suffocating and controlling. It depends on what else is happening and what the context of their relationship is. Are they dating? Are they acquaintances? Is he bullying her?

Experiencing the Planes

It will make a difference for you to experience these spatial arrangements rather than just understanding them conceptually.

Once you experience these spatial arrangements, they will be with you for the long term, like the moment you discover balance when riding a bike. Once the experience is discovered, you won't have to work hard to remember it. It will be there for you to utilize or not—it will become embodied. This spatial understanding will become distinct for you as a powerful tool to enhance and shift your verbal and nonverbal communications. I highly recommend you take on the practices described at the end of this chapter to help you discover the power of space and how it communicates.

To experience the power of the sagittal *High Noon* or confrontational spatial arrangement:

- Have a partner stand in front of you at a distance of about ten feet. Have them walk up to you slowly, and when they get close enough for a conversation, put your hand up to stop them.
- See if you can feel the distance close as it is closing, and feel how your experience of space shifts. Try not to interpret or bring an understanding of the distance as "close enough," and instead, allow yourself to discover the "close enough" distance through sensing it.

The majority of us raised in North America will stop the opposing person at arm's length. This will be the sweet spot in this spatial plane—not too far and not too close—and coincidentally, we will also be close enough to easily grab each other. Another inch or two closer and we will begin to feel uncomfortable or awkward and need to avert our gaze or turn our heads. If we hold eye contact and stand face-to-face, we will likely end up in either a kiss or a fight because being face-to-face and close is both intimate and intimidating. Whether it is intimate or intimidating will largely depend on your relationship to the person and the context of the situation. I enjoy being face-to-face and closer than arm's length to someone I am dating, and someone I am sparring with in the context of martial arts. I do not enjoy being face-to-face and closer than arm's length with a stranger on the subway. When I tie the white belt for a first time student I avert my gaze from their face as I focus on the task. Once it is complete, I stand back or step to the side and look at them before giving a directive or asking any questions. This is one way I use space to manage the dynamics of an interaction. You can also use space to actively impact your experience in interactions as well as the experience of others.

Anthropologist and author Edward T. Hall gives us further insight into why we are generally comfortable at an arm's length in our North American culture in his article "A System for the Notation of Proxemic Behavior." He says that our experience of what is comfortable has a lot to do with being at a distance where we cannot easily smell each other. The closer we get to each other, the higher the probability of smelling each other's body and breath. This increases the level of intimacy. He adds to that the fact that altering the distance between you and another person will also require that you raise or lower your voice and will require that you alter the energy it takes to communicate or impact the level of intimacy as the distance changes. It takes more energy to raise the volume of your voice when you speak to someone outside arm's length, and the lowering of your voice, when someone gets closer, suggests a level of intimacy or secrecy that may not be comfortable or appropriate.

In regard to your safety, the takeaway here is that we are comfortable being with and speaking to most people, even strangers, within grabbing distance, and that being within grabbing distance won't feel weird or too close. Engaging someone in conversation is one of the easiest ways to approach them and therefore get close enough to grab or strike them. These initial conversations are great opportunities to practice saying no non-verbally. When they are engaging you in conversation, you can step or shift or turn away. Both would be nonverbal no's. Or you could stop them verbally and ask them to back up, or practice telling them to stop outside grabbing or striking distance as they are approaching you.

I practice this regularly as I move about my day when I am approached by strangers. Mostly they are innocent requests for directions or money or solicitations for worthy causes. My actions to stop someone before they get too close are frequently met with a startled surprised look and an abrupt stop. I hold out my hand about chest height to indicate that the person should stop. I don't usually need to say anything, but I will often follow up the gesture by saying something like "That's good right there." The action itself is a clear enough communication that most people get it and stop. This gives me a moment to assess and decide whether I want to interact with the person, and I usually do. Once I see that they have respected my boundary by stopping, or even taking a step back-ward, I am free to change my mind, and I can step forward to close the distance. If they don't stop, I have evidence that this person is not listening to me and potentially trying to harm me, and I have discovered that outside of grabbing distance, giving me more time to respond and either to prepare for a fight or to escape. This is a perfect way to practice managing space under normal life circum-stances so that you can build a new muscle for stopping people that you can use when you are more afraid or concerned for your safety.

You can also practice managing space verbally and nonverbally with people you know and trust, when they are standing close to you or if they approach you quickly, in any situation where you feel safe and like you can practice.

To experience the power of the horizontal plane and the "we" spatial alignment:

- Have your partner stand to the side of you at a distance of about ten feet. Have them approach you by sidling up to you, and stop them when they are close but not too close.

- See if you can feel the distance close as it is closing from the side, and feel how your experience of space shifts. Try not to interpret or bring an understanding of the distance as "close enough," and instead, allow yourself to discover the "close enough" distance through sensing it. For most of us this will be right up beside us but not touching. Let yourself experience the oneness with the other person in this side-by-side spatial alignment, the sense that you are not alone, that you are on the same side. This is the spatial alignment and experience of "we."

- To get a sense of how close you are, swivel in to face your partner without changing the placement of your inside foot. Now, likely standing nose-to-nose, you can really appreciate how close you are and how close you are willing to be with a stranger when you are in the plane of "we."

In this plane of alignment, we are closer than we would be if we were face-to-face—usually just an inch or so apart. The reason it doesn't feel too close is because you are not face-to-face.

Aligning yourself in the plane of "we" is a great action to take in a conversation when you find yourself on the opposite side of a point of view and are trying to understand your partner. Go stand beside them. Try to see what they are saying from their point of view. The change in location from a confrontational or positional stance can often open something up in the conversation. At the very least, you will communicate that you are willing to view life from their point of view. In regard to your safety, the takeaway here is that you will let someone get very close to you as long as they are not face-to-face, and it won't feel too close, even though in actuality you are very close to one another. This isn't a problem, but it is something you want to be able to notice.

To experience the power of the 45-degree sweet spot:

- Have your partner stand with their feet side-by-side and facing forward. Stand facing them on an angle directly off their shoulder.

- You will both likely notice that the distance doesn't feel too close, but in reality, you are pretty close. This is because you are not directly face-to-face as you were in the sagittal plane, the plane of confrontation. You may even experience feeling taken care of or supported in this alignment because of the embracing nature of the position.

It is important to note that if placed correctly, you will also have unnoticeable access to the back of their body with your arm while still being able to engage them in conversation. In regard to your safety, you want to be able to notice this 45-degree alignment, especially when someone is using it on you, because it means that they have access to the back of your body, and you won't necessarily see it.

When we do this exercise in our workshops, we have pairs stand in this alignment, and then tell the person who is standing straight ahead (that is, being dominated by the other person's 45-degree position) to find a way to nonverbally say no to this alignment. This will often prompt them to step back or shift their alignment to the person standing off their shoulder. We say that if the person on the 45-degree angle then steps closer to you after this nonverbal no, that person is not listening to you, or potentially is not very spatially aware. Either way, it's useful information for you and how you might want to move forward in the interaction.

REFLECTION AND PRACTICE

The following is an exercise that you can do on your own in your home or in your day-to-day life to experience different ways of paying attention to your environment and to practice being alert and communicating to others the "doing" of being alert. Most of us, at least from time to time, experience being afraid or uneasy while walking alone or in a new place. We fear being followed or jumped from behind. Try this exercise in your everyday life and note how the different approaches to traveling and paying attention to space in the following paragraphs provide different insights.

The Setup: Be in an environment where you can comfortably walk around. This could be an open room or outside while you're going about your day. Make sure your environment is safe for you to move around.

Navel Gazer: Begin by walking around and paying attention only to your inner space. Whatever thoughts are happening, don't try to do anything with them; just let them be there. Check in with your emotions: Are you sad, or irritated, or joyful and excited? What body sensations are present as you move? Are you noticing any aches and pains in your joints and muscles? Maybe your stomach is gurgling with pangs of hunger. Are there any memories present? What would you say is your overall mood or attitude? Are you elated and hopeful or resigned and cynical? Pay attention to any or all of these aspects of your inner space, your internal world. Don't pay attention to anything else outside you. Not the walls or contents of the room or the environment you are in, nor the pets or people who may be near you. Only pay attention to you and your world. Is there a particular posture that comes with this focused attention on your inner world? Maybe you shrink a little or drop your gaze and round your shoulders? Maybe the pace at which you are moving speeds up or slows down? This may be the same posture that you assume when walking with your headphones on while listening to music or when texting on your phone. Do this for at least one minute or however long it takes for you to fully immerse yourself in your inner world.

Tourist: Now, continue walking and replace paying attention to your "inner space" with observing the surrounding environment. Notice as much as you can about the details of the room. Let yourself be fascinated by the light fixtures. Are they clean or dirty, modern or vintage? What color are they? See the furniture as though you are seeing it for the first time. Inspect the colors and textures and design. Make sure you spend some time looking at the ceiling, and check out that smoke alarm. Bring a sense of wonder to all that you behold in this mundane world. If you are doing this exercise outside, bring this same exploration and investigation to that environment. Notice the trees—but really notice them. Notice the variations of color on the leaves, the way they move in response to the slightest breeze. What about those clouds? Are they moving steadily, forming recognizable shapes, and then quickly shifting and disappearing, or is the sky blue with the promise of peace and ease? What else is there? Cars? Other people? Children playing, or adults on their way to work? Keep being curiously engaged as you notice again the posture that arises naturally with this engagement. Did you open up? Has your walking pace sped up or slowed down in response? Do this for at least one minute, or however long it takes for you to fully immerse yourself in your surrounding environment.

Commuter: Now stop. Pick a point directly ahead of you and go directly to that point. It can be in the room you are practicing in, or up ahead if you are outside. Now pick a new point. Again, go directly to that point. Repeat this action for a third time. Once again, bring your awareness to your posture. Has it altered with this course of action? Have you slowed down or accelerated your pace? Do this for at least one minute or however long it takes for you to fully experience moving from point A to point B as directly as you know how.

- What did you discover in this series of exercises about your experience of self-awareness, and the awareness of your environment, and your experience of alertness?

- Which one of these types of paying attention do you think is the best Self Offense and communicates no? Why?

- Which one is most likely to aid you in seeing trouble coming and also not being picked as a target in the first place? Why?

In our workshops, when we ask participants this question, the answer often splits down the middle between the Tourist and the Commuter, because the Tourist is obviously paying attention to their surroundings, and the Commuter walks straight ahead with certainty and confidence; all are valuable qualities in communicating alertness and warding off unwanted attention. Occasionally someone will point out that paying attention to yourself, your thoughts, and how you're feeling (the Navel Gazer) is valuable information for staying safe, and the point is well taken. But on its own it is insufficient. Any one of these ways of paying attention, by itself, leaves you vulnerable and open to attack. The Navel Gazer looks like you are not paying any attention to your surroundings, and it lacks the sense of purpose that the Commuter exhibits in spades. The Commuter creates an impression of confidence and certainty, but the single focus leaves you vulnerable to an attack from behind. The Tourist has the advantage of looking like you are actively paying attention to your surroundings, but it lacks the appearance of confident directness that is the Commuter. This leaves you easy to approach from any side that you are not currently facing. Said another way, it leaves you, at any given moment, vulnerable from at least three sides. All these qualities, the pros and cons, are observable to anyone watching with or without an intent to approach you.

The best Self Offense—the way of paying attention that makes you look the most alert—is a combination of all three.

- Check in with yourself so that you are connected to what's happening with you.

- Know where you are going so that you appear confident in where you are going by going directly there.

- Notice as much of your environment as you can along the way. And don't be subtle about it: Move your head to look side to side. Be obvious about it: Turn around. You want it to be clear to anyone observing you that you are paying attention.

Remember, someone who is paying confident attention to their surroundings is someone who is less likely to be easily preyed on. They may be trained to defend themselves, as they are alert and ready to respond. When you move through your environment appearing confident—moving directly while paying obvious attention to your surroundings—you lower the chances of being chosen as a target. You are subtly communicating that you are not going to be easy to sneak up on, and that you may well be someone who will put up a fight.

The Importance of Turning Around

If you are like most people, you don't have a practice of looking behind you when you are walking in a dark parking lot, or down an unfamiliar street, or before you put the key in your front door. You may not even have a practice of looking behind you—at all.

It's awkward, weird, and sometimes a downright scary action to take. At best, you might glance over your shoulder and consider that looking behind you. The next time you're walking around your neighborhood, or at the grocery store, try looking behind you. Notice whether you stop and glance or whether you turn all the way around.

Take the case that anyone who attacks you from behind is a coward because they are fundamentally unwilling to face you in their attack. They are unwilling to put themselves in that confrontational position. If you did the exercises in the "Plane of Confrontation or Negotiation" section above, you have already experienced for yourself the power of face-to-face interactions. While the situation or circumstances of being attacked face-to-face will be different from walking up to someone and standing face-to-face, as you did in the exercises, the arrangement in space is the same, and the impact of the power of that alignment is still relevant. Being face-to-face under any circumstance is impactful and powerful, and it communicates. Your willingness to turn all the way around to look behind you communicates that you have courage, even confidence, because you are choosing to be face-to-face with a stranger and a potential threat. This makes you potentially a poor choice for attack. Whether you are internally confident or feeling courageous isn't important. In the eyes of the person looking to attack you, turning around to face them communicates that you could easily be someone who makes a scene by yelling, puts up a fight, or has some real combat training. Also, when you turn around to look behind you, they lose the element of surprise, and can now be identified, thus increasing the inherent risk of choosing to attack you.

Turning around to look behind you is something you will likely have to practice more than once and over a period of time.

And if you are too afraid or uncomfortable to turn around and look behind you, and you suspect that there is someone following you, you can walk in a zigzag pattern, and glance over each of your shoulders as you continue moving in the zigzag, like horses do. This will give you a full view behind you as you switch between your shoulders.

A practice that we encourage in our workshop is what we call "the candy cane peel-off." This is like making a U-turn in a car. When you sense someone close behind you, or have a concern that you are being followed, you step off to the side by making a turn in the shape of the curve of a candy cane. If you do this correctly, you will wind up standing in an athletic stance, with one foot forward and one foot back, facing the path you just left and off to your follower's side—perpendicular to them. In addition, you can raise both hands and either press your palms together in a prayerlike position, or hold your palms open and forward at shoulder height, as if to say "Excuse me, my bad." This position is nonconfrontational, and your hands are also up and near your face for protection, in a prime position should you choose to attack to defend yourself. This also removes you from their direct pathway and allows the person walking behind you to either continue walking or forces them to stop, turn, and address you face-to-face. Again, we assert that people who attack from behind are cowards, so arranging yourself face-to-face but off to their side, instead of turning around directly to face them in the original path, the plane of confrontation, avoids communicating a direct challenge while also communicating no. This might be enough for the person either to realize they were following you accidentally and apologize for having gotten close enough to alarm you, or in the case of a potential attacker, cause them to think twice about attacking your confident self.

Eye Contact: Make It or Break It?

Eye contact is such a small thing, and yet it is one of the single most powerful ways to connect with another human being in the shortest amount of time. There are many conflicting opinions about when and where to use eye contact in the context of personal protection.

"Don't make eye contact, you'll invite an attack."

"Make sure to stare them down; show them you're not intimidated."

"Make eye contact; that way you'll be a real person to them, and they won't want to harm you."

"Whoever looks away first is less powerful."

I didn't know what to believe until I began experimenting with the use of eye contact as a martial artist and movement analyst, and then in our Self Offense workshops. A few things became immediately clear: In the moment that you look someone in the eyes, a connection begins. The longer you hold eye contact, the more intimate and related the experience. That prolonged exposure to eye contact can be the most beautiful, intimate, sexy exchange; or the most scary, creepy, or threatening communication. No matter how you slice it, holding eye contact is never boring.

In regard to "looking away first," I have discovered that this belief is not entirely accurate. For instance, if I look at you and something about how you look back at me *causes* me to look away, then I might experience a loss of power. However, if I look at you and then look away when I am ready to look away, I do not experience a loss of power. My ability to both look at you and then look away when I am ready to look away is what contributes to my experience of having power, control, and adaptability in a situation. In other words, if I look away on my own time, I don't experience a loss of power, even if I look away first. If I react to someone's presence or actions by looking away, I do feel a loss of power, or at the very least, I am clearly avoiding the intimacy or intimidation of that engagement. I experience this loss of power when I get caught looking or staring at someone, or if I am forced or made to look away by something in the other person's gaze that makes me uncomfortable.

In our Self Offense workshops, we practice and explore different types of eye contact. When we practice making and holding eye contact for two to three seconds, there are ripples of laughter, giggling, and comments as people connect with each other. Then we shift the exercise to glancing at each other furtively, either to avoid eye contact altogether or not to be caught looking at each other. There is, at worst, a sense of uneasiness and distrust in the room, and at best a "to each their own" kind of separateness present. Finally, we have people practice combining the two by making brief eye contact—a split second or a second long—and then looking away with a quiet mantra of "I see you and I am saying no to you" as they look away. With this third eye-contact option, what emerges in the group is a kind of quiet confidence. People are confident to see others and be seen themselves. The change in the dynamic of the room from one version of the exercise to the next is palpable. Eye contact communicates!

Ultimately, making or breaking eye contact can be a powerful tool to communicate availability or unavailability, confidence, and awareness. Sometimes it's a good idea to make eye contact and sometimes it isn't. This will depend on the context and the circumstances of the situation, and it will depend on you. Remember, you're the expert in any situation in which you find yourself.

For many people the willingness to make or break eye contact will vary with the situation. In some environments or situations, or with certain people, eye contact will be easy or desired and, in others, it will be awkward or uncomfortable, like when you are among strangers or if you have something to say that you are afraid or uneasy to say. For most of us, we will notice that we either have an overall preference for seeking out eye contact and being direct, or a preference for avoiding it or being indirect or covert.

Those of you who seek out eye contact tend to appear available and easier to approach, which you could say is the downside in a personal protection context. On the other hand, your probing or inquisitive stares might make others nervous or uneasy and be read as intimidating. As someone who is comfortable making eye contact, you may find that you are often approached by strangers for directions, or by panhandlers for money, or you get stopped to fill out surveys and join causes—it's just easier to get your attention. On the plus side, your willingness to make eye contact or scan faces can alert you to potential dangers from a safer distance. Another plus side of making eye contact is the potential to hold people with your eye contact. Remember interactions with a parent, sibling, or teacher: All they had to do was give you *that look,* and you heard loud and clear in the silence, "Don't even think about it." Your ability to make eye contact from afar can also be effective in holding people at a distance.

Those of you who avoid eye contact, or at least don't seek it out as a preference, generally read as harder to approach or unavailable. In a personal protection context, you could say this is the plus side. This also means you are less likely to have to deal with random conversations or strangers approaching you to interact. The downside is that not making eye contact can be interpreted as you being rude or scared, and for sure you are missing out on the opportunity to assess the people in your environment from a greater and safer distance.

From the perspective of Self Offense, we invite you to explore all types of eye contact so that you can have them as tools to use in the variety of interactions and situations you may find yourself in, threatening or not. When it comes to protecting yourself, and in particular, managing eye contact with strangers, I invite you to practice the third eye-contact option, combining looking at people for a moment and then looking away: "I see you and I am saying no to you." It communicates both the confidence and the certainty of "I am willing to look at you" and "I see you," and am therefore potentially too much trouble to attack, with "I am a no for being interacted with or approached," making it more difficult to get your attention.

It is important to note that once you establish a momentary relationship through eye contact—looking for more than one second—you may have to work a little harder to communicate the no that follows that eye contact: A moment ago you were communicating yes, and as we saw in the examples above, there are a lot of conflicting ideas out there about what eye contact means. Working harder to communicate no could look like staring at something that is not them, or intentionally not looking at them. It could also look like turning away, shifting your body language, or even saying something: "Stop staring, dude." Anything that reinforces your no and works for you in that situation is a valid choice and will help clarify that there has been a shift in your availability or willingness for interaction.

Sometimes, eye contact is not warranted or seems too risky, but you can still keep someone in your awareness without inviting them to engage with you. The following examples, from people who have taken the workshop, illustrate this. Both take place on the subway, but they could be in any public setting where people are waiting, like an airport or a shopping mall.

I got on the subway, and as I was finding my seat, I noticed an angry, muttering character across the aisle. It felt too confronting to look him in the face, like that might provoke him to be even more aggressive. I sat down and kept my eyes on his shoes. I figured that keeping an eye on his feet would keep me safe by giving me plenty of notice if he stood up and started to head my way. It worked like a charm, and at the next stop I changed subway cars.

■ ■ ■

I was on the subway alone late at night last month, which is an especially nerve-wracking thing to do nowadays, and a woman walked between the cars and started asking for money. When someone told her no, she would yell at them and get close to their face before moving on to the next person. While she was walking down the car, she and I made eye contact. I straightened my back and looked at her for a second before looking away, trying to imitate the "I'm looking at you, and now I'm done with you" stare that Zelda does in one of the TikToks. By the time she came to me, we made eye contact again before I looked away, and she kept walking. I was the only person in the car she didn't directly approach. She likely wasn't dangerous nor had any intention of real harm, but it was a relief that I was able to steer her away from me using just my body.

REFLECTION AND PRACTICE

Notice in your everyday life how you use eye contact. Do you avoid it? Do you initiate it or seek it out? Is it comfortable and easy or is it awkward?

- Overall, are you someone who prefers making eye contact or prefers to avoid making eye contact?

- In what situations or scenarios do you notice that you seek out eye contact?

- In what situations or scenarios do you notice that you avoid eye contact?

- What comes up for you when you make eye contact? What thoughts, feelings, body sensations, or memories are triggered?

- Are there specific relationships in which you notice a preference for making or avoiding eye contact? Why?

Begin practicing eye contact or looking directly at people, and then calmly avert your gaze from a safe distance. As you get more comfortable with this kind of interaction, you can practice with people in closer proximity. It will give you the experience and the appearance of being confident and certain of yourself and aware of your environment.

You can even practice holding people at a distance with your gaze. I practice this by saying to myself: "I see you, and now I am done seeing you." I always feel powerful when I do this. Try it—see what it does for you.

Tip: If you experience discomfort looking someone directly in the eyes, try shifting your gaze to look just above their eye level— more in line with their eyebrow. It will still feel to them that you are looking at them while taking away some of the intensity of direct eye contact.

7

Time and Pressure

Many of our day-to-day disagreements and conflicts can be boiled down to an insistence that life unfold at the pace of our choosing. This inherent need to dominate the pace of life can be found as either a driving force or a subtle but powerful undercurrent in any disagreement. This chapter offers some practices to recognize and utilize the role that time plays specifically in the context of Self Offense but also in your life. While we all get the same twenty-four hours in a day, our experience of time is completely subjective and, what's more, we expend considerable effort to have other people either speed up or slow down their actions to match our preferred (at least in the moment) approach to time. And when things don't happen within the frame of time that we think they should, there is often upset or discomfort.

The dimension of time, experienced firsthand as both an observable phenomenon and a direct personal experience, was first introduced to me in my Laban studies. For instance, there is a big difference between someone moving quickly and someone moving with acceleration. Moving quickly is a comparison to the speed that someone or something else is moving. Acceleration is moving faster and faster over a usually short period of time, and it's most easily observable in explosive beginnings, like the start of a race, or an abrupt ending, like the final moment of impact in a punch.

I began to experience my own preference for Quick Time—accelerating in short bursts—when the group was given an exercise to advance in a straight line toward the other side of the room, and we were told to do it with sustainment, or Sustained Time, savoring each step as though it was the most delicious step ever, so delicious that we never wanted it to end. I nearly lost my mind trying to embody this directive. I felt desperate to get to the other side of the room, to complete the goal. I had all kinds of opinions about why this was the dumbest way ever to approach life. Who would want to take all this time to get a goal accomplished? Especially when they could see the goal and it was so easily accomplished by moving quickly? This became a powerful insight in my life. I saw myself rushing through my tasks just to cross them off my list. It was my competitive nature, and the desire to be the first one finished. I prioritized speed, and it was an overall approach to how I lived my life.

This is an exercise that I have adapted for the Self Offense workshop where we experience the polarities of Quick Time and Sustained Time as a group. I also began to see the important role that time played in some of my recurring conflicts and upsets, as is evidenced in the story below.

My ex-husband and I have different approaches to time in different situations. For example, for many years I competed in martial arts tournaments. Often the tournaments were in nearby states, requiring that we rent a car. My ex insisted on driving the posted speed limit, while I thought of the speed limit as more of a suggestion than a rule. I needed to get where I was going and get there quickly! I sat beside him in the front seat, and I swore that we were crawling along in traffic. All the other cars were zipping past. I looked longingly at them and got more and more anxious and upset that I was going to be late. I was going to miss my event. We inevitably ended up in some kind of spat, with me accusing him of undermining my efforts or not caring enough about what I cared about. Contrast this with any time we walked somewhere together. My ex was a quick walker, and I liked to take my time, stopping to savor the sparkly shiny offerings in store windows. This would often lead to arguments, with me accusing him of being impatient or uninterested, and him accusing me of wasting time.

Once I realized my preference for Quick Time, and I could take responsibility for my need to be the boss of time when we traveled by car, we stopped fighting. I also got to see that he preferred to walk quickly to reach his destination and I preferred a more savoring approach. Once we saw that, we had the option to verbally negotiate the time we took together or agree to arrive separately.

Not only do people have preferred approaches to time, those approaches can vary in different situations. A common way to experience control in a situation is to attempt to control the time in which the experience unfolds. That is perfectly ordinary, and we rarely have the same approach to time as the other people in our lives. I would go as far as to say that it is so rare that when it does happen, it leaves us with an unmistakable experience of elation and a sense that all is well or being dealt with powerfully and effectively. To give you a sense of how different situations and relationships impact our approaches to time, and what it might look like when you and others' approaches to time are not aligned, let's do an exercise in imagining.

- Picture yourself as a parent or caregiver hurrying your child to get dressed and out the door, only to find yourself yelling after them to slow down and walk with you once you hit the street.

- You impatiently tap your foot as you stand fully dressed and ready to go while your partner is ever so slowly sitting down to tie one shoe, and then the other. They get their coat on, and all the buttons done up, and then they have to pick out the right hat.

- You are at work, rushing to make a deadline, and a coworker stops by your desk to share with you a long drawn-out account of last night's escapades. They probably aren't out to sabotage you; maybe they have all the time in the world and you don't.

In each of the above examples, the approaches to time are out of alignment, and that creates a particular experience that is disjointed. Whether it creates stress, anger, upset, or weirdness, something is fundamentally off, and often it doesn't feel good.

One way we experience agreement and alignment, or a sense of getting along, is when we agree, consciously or not, to align on the time in which the experience unfolds. For instance, when we are all in a hurry together to get a project completed or get out the door in the morning, or we are all slowing down together to indulge in an after-dinner stroll or a multicourse meal. This alignment feels good: We are on the same page. It doesn't matter which kind of time it is, Quick Time or Sustained Time; it matters that we are aligned in our approach to time.

But what does this have to do with Self Offense or protecting yourself? Consider the scenario in the stairwell described in chapter 1. The person who assaults Kelly is in a rush. He speaks to it when he says, "We don't want to be late," and "Let's not just stand here." He is in a rush because he is in a vulnerable location. The stairwell of the apartment is a public place where anyone can walk in at any moment. It is in his best interest to move Kelly to a second location as soon as possible. In contrast, she is being cautious and hesitant and is in no rush to go anywhere with this stranger. He is using language to hurry her along, and she may be experiencing pressure, or that time is of the essence. This sense of pressure to move at his pace interferes with her stopping the action or taking her time to investigate further his presence in the building.

As an important aside, one of the first laws of safety is not to go to a second location. The second location is always better for the person who intends harm and worse for the person potentially receiving harm. You may need to expand your definition of a second location. I don't mean New York City to Los Angeles or even Brooklyn to Queens.

Consider that a second location could include moving from the hallway outside to the apartment inside, or the street to the car, or the bar to the street, or the living room to the bedroom. If an altercation goes down, you want it to go down where you have the best chance of being seen and heard by others. We say that the first potential for a fight happens verbally, and while we want to avoid physical altercation, if Kelly had stuck with her no and refused to move from the first location of the stairway, her attacker would have had to choose between giving up or escalating the attack or his insistence that they change locations. In turn, that may have given Kelly the evidence she needed to keep him out of her home. Kelly likely felt safer in her apartment than in the hallway, which is an easy mistake to make.

But back to time: Time is hidden in plain sight in our language. "I'm so impatient." "What's the rush?" "They are/I am quick to anger, or lazy, or always late." "Hey, relax. Be chill." "Take your time. No rush." "They are/I am slow as molasses." "Moving at a snail's pace."

One of the ways that we communicate urgency and emergency is by communicating through the expression of quick or sudden time. "Let's go, now," "Hurry up," or by fast-talking or moving quickly while urging or demanding others to join us at that pace. This can create drama and even an anxious or panicky reaction in ourselves and in others.

Zaylor's story, below, illustrates how you can own your approach to time, and how that ownership can reduce stress and conflict in your life.

Zaylor's Story

Zaylor, a successful entrepreneur and relationship coach, attended one of our workshops in 2017. Before taking the workshop she confided in me that she deals with anxiety—some of it related to past traumatic experiences and some it she attributed to a more generalized experience of life.

The time exercise happens toward the end of the workshop when a good sense of trust has developed in the group. We begin the exercise by having participants walk around the room and ask them to become aware of their own experience of time in that moment. Are they feeling slow, or sluggish, or tired, or are they feeling well rested and perky? We then encourage them to reflect on their lives. What conversations do they entertain about themselves in relationship to time? Do they relate to themselves as slow-witted, or impatient, quick to judge, or super laid-back, or are they generally challenged or victorious when it comes to time management? Next, we direct people by chasing, stomping, clapping, and yelling at them to experience being late—really late, at the level of emergency, until they are madly racing around the room in an effort to catch up. From there, we abruptly shift gears and give all the participants all the time in the world to get where they are going. There is no urgency, no rushing; in fact, we say things like, "If we never get there, no problem," "If this were a race, the last one to arrive would win." They are to savor each step they take, make it last, draw it out as long as possible.

During the exercise, Zaylor first noticed being annoyed and anxious when she experienced being made to hurry up or rush. This was a familiar experience of having to keep up with others, and it triggered a fear of being left behind. When she looked beyond her annoyance and anxiety she saw that she had been told to rush—like going fast is better—for most of her life. And it never occurred to her that this was a *possible* way to go through life, not the only way or the best way. When the exercise shifted and she could savor her walking around, she saw that she wanted to expand that space to give herself the time she wanted and needed, and that she could give herself permission to take her time, and it didn't mean she was less than or broken in some way. She could in fact be deliberate and methodical and thorough when she moved at this pace, and that was a valid and even preferred way of approaching many tasks. She could see her savoring, sustaining approach to tasks as a preference, and once she saw it as a preferred approach to time, she was free to take that approach or not. Now when someone in her life hurries her along, she doesn't react like she is doing something wrong by moving at her own pace. She is free to speak to the issue of time itself rather than make it mean anything about her or the other person. Upsets that used to happen with her wife, whose approach to time is often quicker than Zaylor's, have disappeared, and there is newly an opportunity to have a conversation to align on the timing of an action or event rather than be a "not good enough person" for not moving quickly, or view her wife as wrong for pushing her.

REFLECTION AND PRACTICE

If you find yourself in a situation where someone seems to be rushing you along or slowing you down, and this is awkward or uncomfortable, you can better assess this person's intentions by finding something to say no to. It could be addressing the time itself by saying something like:

- "You seem to be in a hurry. Why don't you go along and I will meet up with you later?"

- "This is going to take the time that it takes. If you need to be there earlier, go ahead, I will catch up."

- "You seem like you have more time for this than I do at this moment. I have to go now. I'll meet you there, or we can pick this up again another time."

This both addresses the issue of time and at the same time serves as your no. You are saying no to the time that they are insisting on.

Whether or not the person has your best interests at heart as they hurry you along or slow you down will be up to you to determine. If you are in doubt, you can always find something additional to say no to and see how they react to your no.

Solo Practice

- Take a few moments before you begin an activity like sitting down to eat a meal or getting ready to go out. Notice whether you are in a hurry, or you are approaching this activity without any sense of urgency, indulging in the experience like you have all the time in the world.

- What are the conversations you have with yourself and others concerning time?

- Are you quick to anger? Slow to get going in the morning? Quick-witted? Impatient? Bored? Are people often trying to hurry you up or slow you down? Telling you to relax or to wake up?

- Notice in what situations or interactions you are working on getting others on your time. Notice as you try to hurry people along or slow them down to match you. Some suggestions might be when you are in line at the bank, the dry cleaners, or the grocery store, or when you are waiting for public transportation or in traffc. What do you say to yourself or others? "Come on, let's go," "Wait your turn," "What is taking so long?" "Don't rush me."

Bonus: Practice with a Partner

Part 1

- Person A has a towel or a T-shirt ready to fold.

- Person B coaches person A to fold the item as quickly as possible. You are in a terrible rush to have this done. You might say things like, "Come on, hurry up, faster, faster, Get the lead out, move it, *let's go!*"

- Person A should ignore the coaching and take as much time as they can to savor folding the item. They can interact with person B verbally or not—for example, "I'm folding it perfectly, enjoying and indulging in how the towel feels against my fingers as I ever so slowly and carefully pick the towel up and put it down again. I am making sure that the fold is perfect. I may even have to do it more than once."

Part 2

- Person B has a towel or a T-shirt ready to fold.

- Person A coaches person B to fold the item and take as much time and care as possible. You have all the time in the world for this to happen. Person A might tell them to "Take their time." "Speed kills." "Enjoy the moment." "Savor each moment." "Caress the material." "See it with your hands." "Fold it perfectly."

- Person B should ignore the coaching and get it done as quickly as possible. They can interact with person A verbally or not.

Part 3

- Person A and person B pick the same approach to time, savoring or rushing.

- Repeat the exercise, aligning or agreeing on the approach to time, with both of you savoring or both of you quickening or rushing.

- You can interact verbally or not.

Part 4

- Take a moment to discuss your experience and insights with your partner. What did you notice as you agreed or disagreed on the time that the activity should take?

- Practice noticing how being in sync or out of sync affects your relationships and putting into practice, wherever possible, mutually agreed-on deadlines. Once we are aware of our own natural timing, we can then notice when someone is trying to dominate or control the timing of our interactions.

8

Throwing Your Weight Around

Many people assume that to be effective at protecting yourself or staying safe in life, you need to be strong, loud, and aggressive—ready, willing, and able to fight. While this may be useful and potentially desirable, it is not the only or even the best way to protect yourself. Consider that there is no one way to be or act that will solve all conflicts safely. Good Self Offense means taking preventative actions that are right for you and good for the situation.

A good place to start is wherever you are. You are the person on the ground in any situation that you are in, and that makes you the expert. That makes you the best judge of what actions to take or not take. You will always do the best you can in the moment. Anything else is "shoulda, woulda, coulda" or armchair quarterbacking. If you could have done it differently, you would have. Period.

Self Offense means using your natural and preferred physical and communication expressions to keep yourself and others safe. That doesn't mean you can't or shouldn't develop and expand new ways of being and acting, or take on new skills for your arsenal; it means that you already have everything you need to keep yourself safe. Take the example of Paula in the following story.

> Paula is about 5-foot-5 and weighs 115 pounds. She is a successful master yoga teacher and entrepreneur. She is beautiful, with long brown hair, freckles, and warm smiling eyes. She floats through life with peace and ease. One day she entered a bodega in New York City with her chai latte in one hand, her little dog tucked under her other arm, and her purse slung over her shoulder. She stops dead in her tracks. There was a young man holding a gun pointed over the heads of several people who were lying facedown on the floor with their hands over their heads— he was robbing the bodega. Without missing a beat, in a sing-songy voice, Paula said to herself, "I don't need to be here." She quickly and lightly turned around, gliding her way out the door.

Perfect Self Offense! Perfect for her in that situation. Did you notice that she didn't yell? She didn't fight? She walked out and called 911. She reacted immediately and in a way that was natural and worked for her. Maybe you would have handled it differently. Maybe you would have leapt upon the attacker's back. Or spoken gently to the gunman to let him know you weren't going to be a problem as you got to your knees to join the others on the floor. Maybe you would have reacted by freezing on the spot and, taking in the scenario, decided it was best to remain right where you were, silent and still. An ability to go along with what is happening, or to be able to be still and quiet when you find yourself in a dangerous situation, can be the very best way to handle it. Kelly, the woman in the scenario from chapter 1, eventually escapes her attacker by sneaking past him, out the door of her apartment and into a neighbor's apartment.

In martial arts, we train our ability to be seen as larger than life, able to intimidate by using strong movements that recruit the whole body from toe to head and include blood-curdling *kiai* or spirit yells. We also train ourselves to be "invisible" through quiet, stillness, and controlled stealthy movements that recruit the whole body for light, quick, and supple agility. Why? Because it's all potentially useful depending on the situation. There is no one-size-fits-all answer to being in life safely.

Lightweight and Strong-Weight Movements

I want to share with you some broad strokes of movement dynamics. Keep in mind that I am oversimplifying a complex field for illustrative purposes and to give you easy access to exploration and discovery.

We are going to begin with the subject of weight. Strong and light weight occur in the vertical dimension. As we move closer to the earth, we experience grounding and strength, and as we move away from the earth, we have greater access to lightness. This is observable in nature, for example when cats crouch low in preparation for a lethal pounce to capture a bird in midair, or in the moment that WNBA star Diana Taurasi crouches to load for her famous jump shot. These examples are both in line with the gravitational pull of the planet. While the opposite is also observable in nature, when feathers float downward with lightness and whales breaching upwards to the sky, these are examples of dis-affinities, and while valid, we are going to set them aside for this book. (If you are interested in going more deeply into movement dynamics, I invite you to check out the Laban Institute for Movement Studies and the resources section of this book.)

Many of you reading this prefer to move through life quietly, lightly, smoothly, floating, gliding, soothing, flicking and poking, sneaking and whispering. You are the natural peacemakers, the gentle giants. If you are on the frontlines, we probably missed you because you are so good at going along with and blending in. If we can see you, it's because you wanted us to. You are a modern-world ninja. You may even have a holding-still practice like meditation or a gliding practice like tai chi. While these movement practices are complex, there is a simplified overall impression that one receives when observing the movement. For example, sitting meditation looks simple and easy enough, but the practice of holding a position over time actually requires a great deal of stamina, strength, and flexibility. Tai chi appears to be soft, gentle, and easy, but it has the potential to produce deadly force when applied in push-hands combat.

There are many of you reading this who prefer to express yourselves using strong weight. You move through the world stomping, punching, slashing, wringing, pressing, and yelling. You are the natural fighters, the gladiators often found on the frontline or the natural advocates and protesters. We see you easily, your presence is known, and you are a force to be reckoned with. You may have practices that allow you to express your preference for strong weight, like boxing or construction work.

If you prefer to use light weight when solving conflict, you will likely need to pair it with persistence. The smallest of hummingbirds hold themselves aloft by beating their wings an average of eighty times per second, in other words, with light persistence. Children are masters at wearing down their adults with lightly spoken "why" questions, or the same request for a sweet over and over again in response to no.

In the context of Self Offense, these lightweight ways of being and acting can be useful to buy time or to avoid a sticky situation altogether, at least in the short term, and that may be all you need to get yourself to safety. For example, if you are dealing with someone who is volatile or who you suspect is unstable, and you need to set a boundary but don't want to escalate, you may find it is a better choice to proceed with lightness by speaking softly with a soothing tone.

The use of strong weight is more traditionally what we imagine as being effective in solving conflict, when saying no or boundary-setting. This is the aggressive, strong, deep-register no that escalates in volume. There may also be a sort of crouching or lowering of the body through the pelvis and legs accompanied by foot stomping or stab-like gestures for emphasis. Imagine a toddler, enraged in a tantrum, stomping their feet.

Contrary to popular belief, being strong and exerting strength is not limited to being used by big strong people. Small and mighty women bearing down during childbirth is a great example of how this is a myth. Another example, and one I will never forget, is the image of a grown man, heavyset, 6-foot-2, walking his very small lap dog on a leash. The dog would scamper to keep up with his human giant until some invisible delight would cause the dog to halt, lower its butt to the sidewalk and refuse to move. The tug of war that ensued between this giant of a man and this teeny yet determined dog was both hilarious and an excellent example of a smaller entity using strong weight to effectively communicate resistance.

Many of you will find yourself somewhere between these two expressions of using your weight in communication and in conflict, but with an overall preference for one or the other. The point is that there is no one way or right way to say no or to set a boundary. Saying no lightly and strongly are both valid and effective communications. "No" said strongly—at loud volume, or with a lowered center of gravity—may only need to be said once or twice. "No" said with lightness—at soft volume and with gentleness—may need to be coupled with persistence. If you know this is going into an interaction that you suspect will require boundary-setting, or you find that arising where you weren't expecting it, you can be newly prepared for what it will take to be heard.

REFLECTION AND PRACTICE

Saying No with Lightness

Light weight is accessed naturally in the upper body—in your arms, shoulders, and upper torso. Up on your tiptoes.

1. Face the mirror. It's best to use a full-length mirror if you have one.

2. Identify your center of lightness, the base of your sternum just above your solar plexus.

3. Practice saying no without saying the word *no*. Say "maybe," "I'll think about it," "I'm good," and so on, and visualize speaking from your center of levity. You might speak in a higher or breathier voice.

4. Practice saying the same thing ten times in a row.

5. Practice saying it as you rise up on your tiptoes. Repeat it again while raising your arms. Say it softly as you raise your

chin. Say it smoothly as you lower your eyes. Say it like you are very fancy, or proper, or genteel. Say it as softly as you like; the only rule is to keep saying it.

6. Experience light weight in your body by putting on some uplifting music, and while seated, perform a chair dance using only your arms and upper body. Or move about the room imagining your head is filled with helium or a string attached to the center of your chest is pulling you forward and up.

Saying No with Strong Weight

Where strong weight is accessed naturally is in your legs. To experience this:

Part 1

1. Face the mirror, ideally a full-length one. Identify your center of gravity, approximately three finger-widths below your navel.

2. Practice saying no directly, commandingly, sharply, or loudly as you visualize speaking from your center of gravity.

3. Practice saying no while stomping your foot. Practice saying it as you jump with both feet. Practice saying it while holding your hands out in front of you like a traffic cop. Turn to the side and practice saying no with a hip check.

Part 2

1. Face a wall an arm's length away. Place both of your hands on the wall. Standing upright, push against the wall, keeping your knees lengthened as you push. Notice your experience. Are

you experiencing a buildup of pressure in your body as you press against the wall? Probably not.

2. Lower your center of gravity by stepping back with one leg and bending your front leg. Now push. Is pressure building up in your body as you press against the wall?

In the second instance, you should notice an increase in your experience of your own strength. You will feel your feet, legs, and torso engage in support of your arms. Arms are good for speed and specificity or targeting, while legs are good for power and strength.

CONCLUSION

Here we are at the conclusion of our journey together. I acknowledge your effort and I trust that you have had some worthwhile insights, and along the way have even discovered for yourself a few good practices to engage in. While this is the end of the book, it can also be the beginning of you living in the world practicing Self Offense. Your personal protection practice is yours to continue to discover and craft as you engage in your life. Allow yourself to struggle, to fail, to question, and do so with as much compassion for yourself and others as you can muster.

Given that it is virtually impossible that any two people will handle the same or similar situations the same way, and equally impossible for you to prepare for all the possible scenarios you might encounter in your lifetime, I invite you to consider that you already have everything you need to go beyond self-defense; that living on the defensive may even be harmful to your health and well-being and will certainly rob you of peace of mind. A final practice could be to give up or let go of the limiting belief that you can't protect yourself. You can, you have, and you are. You can be in life connected to what is happening as it is happening—that is, what is being said *exactly* and what actions others are taking that are *observable.* Let your experience shine a light, and practice being a fly on the wall—ask yourself, "What am I seeing and hearing?" Let that reality inform your choices, not what you think may or may not happen.

While it may seem obvious, it's worth being reminded that this is your life and you get to say what you are willing to fight for. You get to say. And when I say "fight," I mean both figuratively and literally. Your arsenal of weapons includes all the ways you express and own your no. This will always be your first line of defense in Self Offense—that is, setting and expressing your boundaries. You get to say where you draw the line at any given moment. If material stuff is important to you, then you may fight to keep your purse from a snatcher or your car from a carjacker. If your body is where you draw the line, then you will fight to keep anything happening to it that is outside your consent. If it seems safest for you to let them steal your purse or treat your body in a way that you don't want, but you are going to fight like hell for your life, then that's where you draw your line. Anywhere you draw the line is valid, and may shift from moment to moment, depending on the circumstances and the context for those circumstances. Own it.

The choices you make will be your choices to make. You will know because you are there, and you know you, and that makes you the expert. The results of those actions may not turn out how you wish, hope, or anticipate, and you will still be able to own your actions, and with that will come an experience of power and learning to carry forward and contribute to others.

The practices that you have learned or explored in your engagement with this material will empower you in any situation, with anyone, anywhere, and at any time. The more you practice protecting yourself and others, the more your responses will be natural.

Now go. Be free. Unleash yourself. Practice saying your no in whatever way *you* say it. Practice noticing and receiving no from others. Set the example. Walk the talk. Be a demonstration of what it looks and sounds like to honor boundaries. This will make space for others to do the same.

ACKNOWLEDGMENTS

In my dojo, we say that no one gets a black belt by themselves. It's not possible; it takes a community. The same thing can be said for a book. Below is the community of extraordinary people and resources that went into the creation of the Self Offense workshops and this book.

Malcolm R. Gay, for your fierce and funny heart and your love of all things "Power Ranger" that first led our family to the martial arts. And especially for the many hours you took care of yourself in my absence; I am proud of you and the man that you have become.

F. Zelda Gay, for your vision, brave intelligence, creativity, and passion for self-expression that continues to inspire the work of Self Offense to new heights. For all the time you give to me and for your deep contributions to this book—editing, writing, and suggesting. Thank you for recreating me.

Broadway Dance Center's International Student Visa Program and Professional Program, headed by Bonnie Erickson, who gave us our start and then provided a regular opportunity for our workshops to develop, flourish, and contribute to the protection of their students, beginning in 2004.

Shihan Gene Dunn, my mentor and teacher, for creating a space for me at the table. For all our great conversations, past, present, and future. I would not be where I am in this journey without your generous sharing of your experience, wisdom, and love.

Richard Burst-Lazarus—your questions were the catalyst for this book. Your work reading and editing this manuscript, and your partnership in creating Workplace Self Offense, Kids On the Offense, and the online versions of Self Offense have been immeasurable and invaluable. And for doing all that while holding space for and capturing the gold in what gets said.

My dearest friends Diane Bank, Dee Martin, and Shona Drysdale Gawronski, who keep me laughing, uplifted, and real.

Mike Lesser, for your commitment to my development and the development of this work, and especially for your honoring of those that the rest of us are quick to punish and dismiss—"your guys": the convicted, the homeless, the addicted, and the neurodiverse.

Ed Lisbe, for listening so lovingly and for your ListenFirst Workshops, which trained us Peace Amazons (the Self Offense Original Team) to do just that—listen first, and then keep practicing.

The Peace Amazons: Jessica Stone, Laura Newman, Lauren Winters, Mallory Galbreath, Marie Rie-Walker, Mariposa Fernandez, Michelle Zaylor, Senpai Tara Bankoff, Trisha Janelle, and Paul Picciani—for your radical compassion, authenticity, and courage as we confronted and made space for the nasty and gnarly side of our humanity. Together we created Self Offense Services, the Our Space Retreat, operation manuals, videos, teacher training, and online training.

For Senpai Stafford Bey Redding O'Brien and D'Angela Lynn Alberty, our social media goddesses, whose ingenuity, creativity, and authenticity catapulted our visibility from thirty-four to over sixty thousand followers and helped craft our message and our "mother-daughter" kooky expression on the internet. This book, quite literally, would not be the same without you.

To the early adopters and those who continue to champion Self Offense and empower my leadership; Senpai Stephanie Lazarus,

Senpai Krista Vezain, Senpai Kylin O'Brien, Senpai Maria Chang, Sensei Diane Bank, Senpai Laura Belsey, Shruti Kapoor, Ritu Chander, Amy Matthews, Aynsley Vandenbrouke, and Tracey White and family; you never lost sight or let me forget what was possible; thank you.

Scott Mason, Iman Khan, Evan Lambert, Sensei David Adams, Gilson Oliviera, Sensei Bob Gay, and all the other men who contributed their perspective, experience, expertise, and support of Self Offense and for your willingness to pass the mic so that the women in your life can be heard.

The SFMAI-Battodo-Taijitsu-Karate-Do Ken Wa Kan community for your ongoing support and for the many times you forgave us for scheduling Self Offense workshops during your regular practice time.

Shihan Maria Van Dessel for your contributions to this book both as a highly trained martial artist and editing eye. And especially for loving and respecting me through the most challenging periods of my career in the martial arts.

Master Andrew J. Hahn, Shigeru (Soshu) Oyama, Shihan Ted Oyama, Shihan Gene Dunn, and Sensei Garry St. Leger for your mastery in the martial arts and your generous contributions to the development of the self-defense portions of the Self Offense workshops.

Red Penguin editor Stephanie Larkin, for your unfailing encouragement, love for writers and words, and your deep bucket of patience.

The work of Rudolf von Laban (L/BIMS) for bringing language to Space, Time, and Weight that is the foundation for the self-awareness practices of Self Offense.

Gavin de Becker, whose book *The Gift of Fear: And Other Survival Signals That Protect Us from Violence* sparked the workshops that became this book.

Landmark Worldwide and the North Atlantic Seminar Leaders for your "transformational badassery." It is in your listening and taking a stand for what is possible that I get to live a created life and contribute that to others. It is through our work together that Self Offense gets to arise in a space of authentic inquiry rather than as another brick in the dividing wall of blame, shame, and righteousness.

Kristi Sesso—my ontological mother—I am forever grateful for your ferocious love and compassion, for showing me what it looks like not to settle for less than what is possible, unpredictable, and miraculous.

My NAB editor, Shayna Keyles, who plucked me from the chaos of social media and inspired me to reach way beyond where I would have stopped in the writing of this book; ensuring that this work has the best shot at making the biggest difference with as many people as possible.

My parents, Gay and Ted Clarke, for giving me my life and then loving me deeply, playfully, and unrelentingly throughout.

My siblings, Tina and Mike: I have not always been easy, and having your love on either side of my growing up has helped keep me true.

This is our book.

RESOURCES AND RECOMMENDATIONS

Websites

Self Offense: www.self-offense.com

Shihan Michelle: www.shihanmichelle.com

Rape, Abuse & Incest National Network: www.rainn.org

New York State Coalition Against Sexual Assault: www.nyscasa.org

988 Suicide and Crisis Lifeline: www.988lifeline.org

Bystander and intervention training, Right to Be: www.righttobe.org

National Sexual Violence Resource Center: www.nsvrc.org

Landmark Worldwide: www.landmarkworldwide.com

Self Offense Podcasts and Videos

The Martial Arts Mind, "Safe and Sound" episode, July 27, 2018, www.martialartsmind.com/new-podcast-episode-20.

Got It from My Mama, episode 108, www.gotitfrommymomma podcast.com/episodes.

NPR *Life Kit,* "3 Personal Safety Tips to Help You Protect Yourself on a Night Out," October 31, 2022, www.npr.org/2022/10/27 /1132016606/how-to-stay-safe-during-a-night-out.

Purpose Highway, episode 5, "Reduce the Risk of Being Attacked," www.gaana.com/artist/how-do-you-reduce-the-risk-of-being -attacked-and.

Tedx, "Ending Sexual Assault: The Best Defense Is a Good Offense," www.ted.com/talks/michelle_gay_ending_sexual_assault_the_best _defense_is_a_good_offense.

Books

Gavin de Becker, *The Gift of Fear: And Other Survival Signals That Protect Us from Violence* (Boston: Little, Brown, 1997).

Edward T. Hall, *The Hidden Dimension* (New York: Anchor, 1990).

Ellen Goldman, *As Others See Us: Body Movement and the Art of Successful Communication* (New York: Routledge, 2004).

Karl E. Geis, *A Book of Twelve Winds: An Aikido Master's Life Strategy* (Houston: Fugakukai, 1992).

Warren Lamb and Eden Davies, *A Framework for Understanding Movement: My Seven Creative Concepts* (London: Brechin, 2012).

Rudolph von Laban, *The Language of Movement: A Guidebook to Choreutics* (Boston: Plays, 1974).

Ram Dass, editor, *Miracle of Love: Stories about Neem Karoli Baba* (Santa Fe, NM: Hanuman Foundation, 1995).

Bruce Hyde and Drew Kopp, *Speaking Being: Werner Erhard, Martin Heidegger, and a New Possibility of Being Human* (Hoboken, NJ: Wiley & Sons, 2019).

Trainings

The Landmark Forum, www.landmarkworldwide.com

Self Offense Online Training on Kajabi, www.self-offense.mykajabi .com/self-offense-online-course

Laban/Bartenieff Institute of Movement Studies, www.laban institute.org

Gene Dunn's Dojo, Brooklyn, New York, www.dunnsdojo.com

Imazaki Dojo, downtown Chicago, www.imazakidojo.com

Kano Martial Arts, New York City, www.kanomartialartsnyc.com

Karate-Do Ken Wa Kan, New York City, www.kenwakan.com

School of Body-Mind Centering, www.bodymindcentering.com

Hotlines

National Sexual Assault Hotline: (800) 656-4673

National Suicide Prevention Hotline: (800) 273-TALK (8255)

Suicide Lifeline: 988

National Domestic Violence Hotline: (800) 799-7233

Social Media

Instagram: @Self_Offense

TikTok: @SelfOffense

Facebook: @SelfOffense

YouTube: @selfoffense

INDEX

ABOUT THE AUTHOR

Shihan Michelle, CMA, R-MPA, is a 6th degree black belt and a six-time World Oyama Women's Knockdown Karate Champion. She obtained a 2nd degree black belt with the All United States Kendo Federation studying Iaido with Sensei Pam Parker at Ken Zen dojo in New York City. She volunteered as a rape crisis advocate for St. Vincent's and New York Downtown Hospital from 1998 to 2004. Michelle graduated from the Laban/Bartenieff Institute for Movement Studies as a Movement Analyst in 2003 and became a Registered Movement Pattern Analyst in 2019. Her passion for movement exploration and her drive to delve deeper into the anatomy of what she teaches in karate led her to complete a total of 140 practical hours of integral anatomy with Gil Hedley at the University of Medicine and Dentistry of New Jersey. This also led her to undertake hundreds of hours studying and embodying developmental movement, embryology and ontological movement, and the various systems of the body with the brilliant, wise, and loving Bonnie Bainbridge-Cohen and her rich web of body-mind centering practitioners and teachers. In 2003 she founded the Society for Martial Arts Instruction as a haven for esoteric martial arts clubs and somatic movement practices. In 2011 Michelle founded the first somatic movement-based full-contact karate school, Karate-Do Ken Wa Kan, in New York City. She currently runs the school, where she trains and teaches alongside her daughter, dear friends, and respected colleagues. On the mat, she is training hard in pursuit of her next black belts in judo and Brazilian jiujitsu.

Michelle is a professional Seminar Leader for Landmark Worldwide and has been leading transformational seminars in person and online since 2012.

The Self Offense: Preventative Personal Protection Program was created in 2004 and, through its various incarnations (Good Guy/Bad Guy, No Way Know How, and Safe & Sound), has been taught to thousands of people ages eleven to seventy-nine in martial arts and movement schools, corporations, diplomatic agencies, and top universities in the United States, India, Sweden, Germany, Canada, and Australia. The core distinctions that make up Self Offense continue to expand and have been adapted to also address children and bullying prevention, de-escalation training, boundaries and communication training, awareness and threat response, and workplace harassment prevention trainings. That body of curricula has additionally served work release and rehabilitation programs, parent and teacher communities, tech and health care companies, children's and family aid organizations, and after-school programs across the United States.

Michelle's first book, *Brain Breaks for the Classroom* was published in 2009 by Scholastic Teaching Resources, and her article "What's Your Next Move: Consult Your Reflexes" was published in the BMCA journal *Currents* and in *Exploring Body-Mind Centering: An Anthology of Experience and Method,* published by North Atlantic Books in 2011. In 2021 she presented "Ending Sexual Assault" as part of the TEDx Cherry Creek Women Event.

Michelle currently lives, plays, and practices Self Offense in Brooklyn, New York. See www.shihanmichelle.com.